Table of Contents

No one can say when the unwinding began—when the coil that held Americans together in its secure and sometimes stifling grip first gave way. Like any great change, the unwinding began at countless times, in countless ways—and at some moment the country, always the same country, crossed a line of history and became irretrievably different.

-George Packer

The Unwinding
An Inner History of the New America, 2013

Prologue

Mid-November, 2009: a moving company was busy packing my most important belongings. The boxes were marked: "Aspen, Colorado."

My condominium in Zurich was going to be rented, and I was on my way to my new home, where I would join my American wife, who was terminally ill and, at that time, was being taken care of by the wonderful staff of a care center. I had been traveling back and forth for the last two years; that December, I was moving for good. Moving to a new country, facing a new culture, and leaving behind a comfortable life full of the familiar faces of family and friends was a challenging undertaking at age 62—a daunting task.

Yes, I was now retired, and I was going to collect monthly incomes from the Swiss Social Security and my pension fund for the rest of my life. The combination of two annuities would allow me to live comfortably, if not luxuriously, in Switzerland or anywhere else in the world.

In 1986, the Swiss citizens, in a popular vote, voiced their approval for a mandatory pension plan dedicated to all working people, payable at their retirement age. According to this plan, both employees and employers pay jointly into Social Security, as well as into the personal pension plan of the employees. The more than 40 years I had paid into my Social Security account may seem a long time. Today, however, I am reaping the benefits of a complete pension fund system.

Eight years since the year of the big move, I am well-settled in Colorado. I am truly enjoying this beautiful country, graced with the mountains and all the joys and adventures this western countryside has to offer. Most of all, I enjoy the friendships I have made, and the many interesting, kind, and wonderful people I have met over time. I call this comfortable lifestyle "freedom" - real freedom, and peace of mind.

While I observe so much wealth and luxury in this tiny Roaring Fork Valley, with probably some of the most expensive homes in the country located in Aspen, I watch some people struggling, working two jobs, and toiling long past the age of 65 just to put food on the table.

Until only a few years ago, immigrating to America was the dream of millions of young people, and *freedom* was the magic word. America was the country where you could make a fortune and create success just by working hard. It was a country of meritocracy and potential prosperity.

America was considered one of the leading nations, in fact— the most advanced country in the world. Decisions and actions taken by American politicians were courageous and expressed commitment to the nation's citizens. Products by American companies were innovative, extraordinary, exceptional, and desired by consumers around the world.

Today, it appears that America has lost its glory.

Why?

* * *

As an economist, I am fascinated by the interrelated mechanism of economics and politics. I devote a fair share of my time to uncovering the reasons for the steady drop in popularity. Why are so many citizen resigned and dissatisfied with American political and economic decision making? I refer to these people as the "silent majority." These Americans do not actively participate in political life, but they do have a clear comprehension of the current situation.

Three political topics have dominated the headlines in America and have strongly influenced economic decision making: employment, the budget deficit, and taxes. In this book, I will analyze these three topics and share my findings on how poverty is created and kept in place by institutional mechanisms. I call these mechanisms "poverty traps".

Traveling the country, I have seen the spectrum between opulence and poverty. I am concerned that the gap between the rich and the poor is getting bigger and bigger.

This country is in crisis.

On the political level, we have reached the dilemma of dysfunctional conditions. The country is divided into two big camps, or mainstreams: conservatives and liberals. Whatever the government suggests and presents to its citizens or its party leaders is rejected and debated with resentment. Comments are negative, unproductive, and do not lead to a positive and constructive future for all.

Many urgent issues are unaddressed by politicians, possibly because discussing them is of no interest to their party, their supporters, or the state. Urgent problems, such as immigration, the national budget, and the infrastructure, are postponed, shelved, or simply ignored, creating further resentment and widening the gap both between parties as well as the citizen.

In this book, *Restore Trust*, I seek to share, objectively, my analysis and my understanding of American political and economic decision-making and the underlying impact on the American people and our democracy. The American people are hardworking, friendly, generous, warm, and welcoming.

My book is an invitation to take a fresh look at the current socio-economic reality. I offer opportunities to create a shift to strengthen our democracy and to promote social legislation.

I dedicate this book to the American people.

Part 1: Economic Thinking Errors

Welfare and Federal Funding

A Divided Nation

The United States of America is today a deeply divided nation. There is a rift between the two main political parties, the Democratic Party and the Republican Party. Supporters of each side vehemently and loyally support their individual parties and candidates, convinced that, somehow, their individual party alone can and will bring about the true change that voters are hungry for.

Three political topics have dominated the headlines in America for years and have strongly influenced economic actions: employment, the budget deficit, and taxes. The question of how the government should spend its money ultimately becomes the central focus of political debates. My analysis focuses specifically on the budget deficit and taxes.

In the ideal scenario, the governing body raises funds through the taxes of various sources and then allocates those funds to the beneficial programs that require this money. This is not the case in the United States today. In reality, the government has found itself in a position where it is paying for more programs than it can afford, given the money it actually raised through these taxes. A short-term solution would be the government transferring funding from one program in order to pay for another. This is not a very sustainable solution in the long-term, since vital programs take a massive hit in funding and funding itself becomes a more unfairly subjective process.

The problem is that the government kept spending well beyond its actual intake. Instead of cutting back on spending and focusing on increasing tax revenue, the government began to borrow in excess of the tax revenue. Since 1985, the U.S. has been a debtor nation.

If the government simply followed political principles that obeyed authentic American values that embodied the old legendary America—e.g. meritocracy, fairness, compassion for one's country and concern for its welfare, etc.—then perhaps the U.S. would not hold its current "debtor" status. Higher tax revenue, for example, would invariably reduce the government's budget deficit; alternatively, lower government spending would reduce the tax burden. As it is, this existing huge budget deficit justifies concern for American citizens.

The debate over the Federal Government's spending is something that certainly separates the Democrats and Republicans. In theory, Democrats are not fundamentally opposed to budget deficits, but for a couple of years now, Republicans have been strictly in favor of managing the budget deficit. Fiscal policy is used to argue, fight, and promote the focus of each party whenever it is convenient.

Over the last three decades, none of the presidents and their administrations, irrespective of party affiliation, have been successful in steering away from increased government spending and in bringing about the repayment of today's immense national debt. The ideal solution to this lies in increasing tax revenue while simultaneously making realistic cuts to programs that would suffer least from losing a little funding.

In their concerted efforts for a balanced budget, the core values and focus of the two parties are clear. Republicans demand that budget items for the poor and elderly be significantly reduced in order to reach a balanced national budget. They want to slash and burn every social program in order to reduce this spending. But on the other hand, they insist on massive increases to their own pet causes, like military spending. All they are really doing is robbing Peter to pay Paul; in the end, there is no deficit reduction. To further complicate matters, Republicans additionally want to lower taxes— particularly for corporations—instead of raising them; there is no net gain there, either. For 2018, a new Republican tax legislation was signed in late 2017 which will reduce the tax bill of large companies significantly. Democrats, on the other hand, firmly reject reductions in social programs and argue for increased taxes to keep programs in place and reduce debts.

Neither party offers a winning proposition.

My proposal differs. A closer look at the American economy, especially from a microeconomic standpoint, demonstrates that the poverty in this country is created, sustained, and kept in place by institutional mechanisms. This is particularly true for minimum hourly wages, the social sectors of healthcare, and senior programs. If we leverage these two problematic social welfare sectors, we can considerably reduce their budget items. Regulations requiring wage increases could decrease welfare spending, which would result in a reduction of income tax.

Poverty and Welfare Programs Are Interrelated

Americans are led to believe that their country is, by its very nature, the "land of opportunity" and that the roads are paved with gold. According to this endless propaganda, anyone and everyone can become a millionaire overnight if they just put forth a little more effort. This could not be further from the truth, given that one-fifth of the population can barely make ends meet and fights fiercely for every penny earned.

Have people given up on the American Dream? It is true that some Americans do work hard and smart and thrive—they have the means. But don't fool yourself that they aptly represent the entire country. Visitors traveling through the America hardly notice the poverty. The big tourist destinations are filled with well-fed and happy, exuberant people living in comfortable or luxury homes, using cheap energy and driving big cars.

Yet, beyond the most prosperous districts and the Hollywood signs, much of America is in the throes of poverty—and, with it, poor health and crime. This has been an ever-present, persisting, and longstanding problem. A fifth of America's population is classified as earning less than the Federal poverty level.

The Federal budget, government revenues, and the taxes paid by American citizens are all used to support people below the poverty line with social programs. While this is a noble approach, it creates a vicious cycle for this group as well as for the taxpayers. It keeps the poor immersed in poverty and it keeps American taxpayers footing the bill.

Optimally, budget relief must begin with fighting poverty.

The modern efforts to combat poverty really began with the presidency of Lyndon B. Johnson. He set out to build what he dubbed "The Great Society" and dreamed of a nation where poverty was no longer an issue. He introduced poverty-fighting initiatives such as Medicare and Medicaid and signed both the Civil Rights Act and The Voting Rights Act. Additionally, he sought to reduce poverty through an improved education system and introduced the Head Start program which emphasized early education.

> „To see clearly, it often suffices to change one's perspective."
>
> -Antoine de Saint-Exupéry
> Author of *The Little Prince*

Johnson aggressively initiated nearly every social program that Democrats and many citizens of our society hold sacred today. To a large extent, these programs were very effective - at least for the short-term. They did initially slash the poverty rate by a full 2/3rds.

The U.S. did not continue down the path of "the Great Society", which would have been possible had Congress implemented a minimum wage law that automatically fluctuated based upon the inflation rate. To this day we have a fixed low minimum wage which sustains an impoverished class of people. For many, these social programs that were created as a temporary stop-gap measure have now become a necessary way of life.

Every ten years, the United States Census Bureau publishes the number of citizens classified as poor and categorizes them by age and social class (e.g. singles and families with children). The Bureau defines inflation-adjusted income levels used to classify poverty. The poverty rate of 22% observed in the 1950s dropped to 11% in 2000 and climbed back up to 15% in 2015.[1] That resulted in forty-six million Americans being put into that category today.[2] In New Hampshire, less than 10% are affected. In 15 states, however, the rate is above 17%. These are staggering figures but, unfortunately, this is the current reality.

The Federal Government sets an annual poverty level, called the Federal Poverty Line, for singles and families.[3] If workers fall below this level with their annual income, they receive benefits in the form of food stamps and are entitled to Medicaid, the national healthcare system, as well as to a number of other programs including the National School Lunch Program, the School Breakfast Program, the Section 8 Housing Program, Earned Income Tax Credit, and more.[4] A fair share of your tax dollars, as an American taxpayer, is geared directly towards the support of these welfare programs.

The Supplemental Nutrition Assistance Program (or "food stamps", as they are more commonly known) was initially tested and implemented during the Great Depression in 1929.[5] It was abandoned in 1943 due to the nation's economic recovery. Ever since President Kennedy reintroduced the program in 1961,

---

[1]   "Poverty in the United States, Frequently Asked Questions," National Poverty Center, University of Michigan, April 23, 2015 (http://www.npc.umich.edu/poverty/#3).

[2]   "Poverty USA," an initiative by the U.S. Catholic Bishops, April 23, 2015. (www.povertyusa.org) http://www.povertyusa.org/the-state-of-poverty/poverty-map-state/#.

[3]   Federal Poverty Level (FPL). A measure of income level issued annually by the Department of Health and Human Services. Federal poverty levels are used to determine the eligibility for certain programs and benefits. www.healthcare.gov/glossary/federal-poverty-level-FPL/.

[4]   Tim Worstall, "Fantastical Nonsense About WalMart, The Waltons And $7.8 Billion In Tax Breaks," Forbes, April 14, 2014.

[5]   Randy James, "Food Stamps," Time Magazine, September 14, 2009.

however, statistical figures on total participation and individual benefits have increased consistently. The results for 2013 and 2014 show record values. CNS News reported that, in 2013, 20% of all U.S. households received food stamps.[6]

Poverty as a Structural Problem: Minimum Wage Creates an Entitlement Society

The first minimum wage law was enacted in 1938 and was incorporated into the Fair Labor Standards Act (FLSA). The FLSA additionally oversaw and created regulation standards for programs like youth employment criteria, overtime pay, and recordkeeping.

As previously stated, this was meant only as a temporary measure to provide some relief and to combat the Great Depression. A steady and permanent minimum wage wasn't enacted until some decades later. The motive to create a minimum wage was to legislate that businesses pay workers a sustainable wage.

Today people who work for the Federal minimum wage of $7.25 per hour cannot make ends meet; they fall into the vicious cycle of poverty.[7] These are the so-called "working poor" who often work at two or three jobs because the local minimum wage of one employer rarely pays enough to make a living. The percentage of multiple job holders has steadily increased each

---

6   Ali Meyer, "Record 20% of Households on Food Stamps in 2013," in
     CNSNews.com, January 21, 2014.
7   The minimum wage set by the Federal Government is at $7.25 per hour
     (since July 2009). Performing work in connection with federal contracts is
     paid $10.35 effective January 2018. In some states, it may be higher.

year. As of 2016, 7.9% of all working Americans work two or more jobs.[8] While some of these jobs demand eight hours a day, some of them are seasonal or part-time. The job security provided is minimal to none, as temporary and seasonal workers are typically the first to be fired in times of economic downturn, and they are rarely offered any benefits. Seasonal employment includes everything from tourism to agriculture and attracts a higher number of migrants and young workers. Food services in schools across the country are impacted by irregular working hours, and the gap of unworked hours and days must thus be filled and compensated by another job to boost income.[9]

Many of these low-paid employees in addition work through temporary agencies, which charge clients up to 30% of their employee wages as their fee or commission. Such an employee actually retains even less money in his or her pocket, and companies are happy to interact with the agencies, since it saves them the trouble, time, and money of scouting for new recruits themselves.[10] The chance for promotion to get a salary increase at this level is almost nonexistent.

People living in rural areas have additional challenges such as distance and transportation. How does a person of rural Kentucky have a chance of escaping poverty when there might typically be 30-miles distance to the nearest job and no means of transportation? The reality is that the costs of attaining such a job outweigh the earnings. The end result has been a growing

---

[8]   Paul Davidson, "The job juggle is real. Many Americans are balancing two, even three gigs," *USA Today*, October 17, 2016.

[9]   Charles Babington, Laurie Kellermann, "In Congress, income inequality comes with breakfast, lunch," *Aspen Daily News* (Associated Press), May 4, 2015.

[10]   FindLaw, "Part Time, Temporary, and Seasonal Employees," 2013.

and permanent group of people who has to live below the poverty line.

People accept shabby hourly wages only because they know they can request supplemental income through government programs. The combination of underpaid minimum wage and supplemental social programs is the birthplace of the entitlement society. Economic consequences are simple and clear: whatever companies pay out in wages is supplemented by the taxpayer. These social programs were intended as merely a stop gap, not as a way of life—and yet this is exactly how they are being implemented in our current society.

In the land of endless opportunities we are not willing to pay the lowest income earner a decent wage, but we tolerate subsidizing them with food stamps and Medicaid. Can you see that we are training people to be entitled to receive government support? We are enrolled in the reasoning that the employer cannot afford to pay more, so we need more entitlement benefits. If the minimum wage issue is not effectively resolved on the political level, we will not be able to combat poverty. This initiative must optimally be taken by the leaders—in our case, our political leaders.

Many large corporations pay the Federal minimum wage to some of their employees. These companies have come under scrutiny as of late. In 2012, for example, an Ohio-based Walmart store with a sizable food department organized a food donation drive for its own employees, resulting in the absurd situation of food-selling employees receiving food from the same customers to whom they were selling.[11] This grossly embodies the fact that

---

[11]   David Morris, "Hey Michelle and Barack: Walmart and Amazon are the Problem, not the Solution," *AlterNet,* May 19, 2015 (The article's title refers to statements made by the Presidential couple lauding the good services performed by Walmart in supplying America's population with

Walmart employees cannot survive on their wages and are, therefore, dependent on receiving aid from the government or third parties. The contribution of tax dollars to Walmart is $3,015 per employee every year.[12] (And note, dear reader, that if I frequently quote Walmart in this book, I use the characteristics of this company as an example. The statements and the conclusions are, however, valid for many American corporations.)

Doug Altner, of the Ayn Rand Institute, writes that people should leave Walmart alone and not demand that it pay fair market wages.[13] Every time Walmart opens a new store, he says, there are thousands of people who apply for jobs. Easy work, relatively secure employment, and the possibility of promotion help the public accept the average Walmart wage of $9 or $10 per hour. However, Altner fails to mention that, in addition, the employees have a right to welfare benefits because Walmart pays them so little. Wage subsidies of about $4.2 billion are paid yearly to Walmart's 1.4 million employees.[14] This subsidy was paid despite the fact that Walmart reported a profit of $121.1 billion for 2016.[15]

---

goods.).

[12] "The Low-Wage Drag on Our Economy, Wal-Marts low wages and their effect on taxpayers and economic growth," Report by Democratic members of the U.S. House Committee on Education and Workforce, [consulted May 23, 2015]. http://democrats.edworkforce.house.gov/sites/democrats.edworkforce.house.gov/files/documents/WalMartReport-May2013.pdf.

[13] Doug Altner, "Why Do 1.4 Million Americans Work At Walmart, With Many More Trying To?" *Forbes*, November 27, 2013.

[14] "The Low-Wage Drag on Our Economy...," *ante*.

[15] Walmart Gross Profit, "Walmart Revenue, Profits - WMT Annual Income Statement" (NYSE:WMT), https://amigobulls.com/stocks/WMT/income-statement/annual

President Barak Obama repeatedly promised to raise the minimum wage during his 2008 election bid. "[We] will further raise the minimum wage to $9.50 an hour by 2011, index it to inflation, and increase the Earned Income Tax Credit to make sure that full-time workers can earn a living wage that allows them to raise their families and pay for basic needs such as food, transportation, and housing," he announced during the campaign.[16] Obama made no further mention of this during the first two years of his administration while enjoying a Democratic-controlled Congress and a mandate from the American people.

In his State of the Union Address in January 2015, however, President Obama again voiced his approval for raising the minimum wage to $10. Many economists welcomed the idea, as the results would have meant additional purchasing power for low-wage earners, thereby benefiting all U.S. businesses. The push for a higher minimum wage, however, fell on deaf ears in the corporate world and Obama did not continue to fight for it.

Some city and state officials, such as in San Francisco and New York, have tried, gradually, to increase the local hourly minimum wage to $15 because the statutory minimum wage does not cover the cost of living in these areas.[17] There are discussions underway in New York City about a sliding adjustment to facilitate reaching that goal by 2018. Minimum wage adjustments to $15 per hour have actually already been reported for 200,000 employees in the state of New York who work for fast-food restaurants that boast 30+ locations.[18] The

---

[16]   Politofact August 29, 2011
[17]   Martin Lanz, "Viel Bewegung bei den US-Mindestlöhnen" [Some moves on the issue of U.S. minimal wages], *Neue Zürcher Zeitung*, May 26, 2015.
[18]   Rashed Mian, "NY Moves toward $15 Minimum Wage for Fast Food Workers," *Long Island Press*, July 23, 2015.

University of California's food service has announced its intention to increase the minimum wage.[19] A system of regionally adjusted, tiered minimum wage rates that are in sync with local costs could likewise develop throughout the country.

Both New York and California want to fulfill workers' demands and thereby enable them to live on the minimum wage income. Expressing the needs of workers in similar situations, a 60-year-old Wendy's employee in Brooklyn reported to *Business Insider*: "If I made $15, I could pay my rent on time, I could put food on the table, I could hold my head up. We have worked so hard to make this happen."[20]

In 2015, solidarity rallies were held in San Francisco and New York, while restaurant franchise holders warned of dismissals and price hikes. When Dunkin' Donuts CEO Nigel Travis declared that raising the minimum wage to $15 was "absolutely outrageous" in his opinion, journalists promptly made mention of his hourly wage of $4,800.[21]

The current federal minimum wage for average working Americans was last raised to $7.25 on July 24, 2009. It has been a full eleven years since any federal raise has occurred.[22] In response, some communities along with 18 states have taken it upon themselves to increase the minimum to $10.00 and $15.00 per hour.

On March 6, 2018, Target announced that it will be raising its minimum wage from $11 to $12 per hour. This company is

---

[19] Lisa Leff and David Klepper, "Higher minimum-wage proposals gain ground," *Aspen Daily News,* July 23, 2015.

[20] David Klepper and Deepti Hajela, "For the first time, a U.S. state may single out one industry for a big wage hike, *Busniess Insider,* July 22. 2015

[21] Mark Frauenfelder, "Dunkin' CEO makes $10 million a year but $15 Dollar minimum wage is 'absolutely outrageous,'" *Boing Boing,* July 26, 2015. http://boingboing.net/2015/07/26/dunkin-ceo-makes-10-million.html.

[22] https://www.dol.gov/opa/media/press/esa/esa20090821.htm

already seeing some positive results. Jed Graham in *Investor's Business Daily* reported that Target officials saw an immediate increase in job applications as well as a 'stronger pool of talent' in response to the announcement.[23]

At first glance it may seem like the Republican idealistic model of letting the market dictate wages really does work. In a further incentive for company based minimum wage increases, Fox Business released a report listing all the additional major companies planning to raise their minimum wage rates in response to Republican Tax Reform that passed in December 2017.[24]

There is a straightforward method to fighting this poverty and sparing the taxpayer from subsidizing salaries, and that is to pay fair market wages. Higher minimum wages will notably reduce poverty and, thus, reduce welfare spending. Would there be short-term repercussions to this, as well? Yes, most likely. Such a change would probably affect the labor market negatively and raise inflation for a short period, but the long-term results would be worthwhile, given that we'd see an end to the vicious cycle of poverty and subsidizing minimum wages.

This vicious cycle appears to be widespread throughout the country. It is typical for American companies to comply with a state's calculated minimum wage and offer little more. The local suppliers of wholesalers are happy to keep their wages at that level, and it is the public purse that subsidizes the workers and keeps them from starving.

23   Jeff Graham, "Target Hikes Base Wage To $12 An Hour, One-Upping Walmart Despite Earnings Squeeze", *Investor's Business Daily*, March 6, 2018, https://www.investors.com/news/economy/target-hikes-base-wage-to-12-an-hour-above-walmart/

24   Thomas Barrabi, "Tax reform windfall: These companies are hiking pay, delivering bonuses", *FOXBusiness*, March 7, 2018

Some argue that boosting the minimum wage to a higher level could be considered a tax on all citizens and businesses. Higher wages would increase product prices. Because no company wants that risk of losing competition, taxpayers are forced to continue supplementing employee paychecks. I declare that this has turned the U.S. into a socialized economy; I'm talking about a socialized economy only as a result of the low wages paid by many corporations. This mentality of paying low wages and complementing them by government social program payments reminds me of the economies of Eastern European communist countries before 1989 when all retail offers were low but subsidized.

As a result, poverty in America is systemic. Poverty is sustained by legal regulations of the too-low minimum wage, which simultaneously increases public welfare spending. The bottom line here is that wage subsidies do not belong in free-market economy. A wage structure that is supplemented by the taxpayer is diametrically opposed to the market principles so often postulated abroad by U.S. economists. Since subsidies are very much frowned upon in this country, I do not understand this blatant distortion of the market economy being overlooked.

In other words, higher wages at the lowest level means a return to a market economy in all industries. If you are in favor of lower taxes and less welfare spending, you have to be prepared to pay more for your purchase at Walmart, or for your morning coffee in a fast-food outlet.

The Republican Party resists higher minimum wages altogether, something that suggests that Republicans are indirectly responsible for increased welfare spending. I personally find this an oxymoron; it is dishonest, absurd, and contradictory to keep minimum wages low and to lament the Federal Government's welfare spending at the same time.

Economically speaking, insufficient income and high welfare spending are interrelated. This is a Gordian knot that needs to be cut to resolve the real economic issues and their impact.

Low wages cost the American taxpayers $152.8 billion each year in federal subsidies for working families.[25] It makes more sense to raise the minimum wage and commit to enforcing a free market mechanism. In the end, higher minimum salaries result in higher incomes, higher prices for products, but as well in lower social costs and lower taxes; the yield is a zero-sum game. The monetary values of business, income, social services, and taxes would furthermore be more transparent.

To demand the dismantling of social services, as some of their critics do, is to turn a blind eye to reality. Fixing the mandatory minimum wage is an intervention into the laws of the free market, but so are subsidies and welfare programs. The minimum pay if set too low, causes the permanent underpayment of workers and, as a result, these jobs will not be filled. It simply does not make sense to accept work for pay that does not cover the real cost of living. Yet many people find themselves with no other choice.

If self-regulation of free-market mechanisms were functioning efficiently, it would not be necessary to set minimum wages at all. In order to allow the market to determine—or even to abandon—minimum wages, unions and other bargaining agents representing the interests of wage earners must be accepted. Ironically, instead of allowing the free market to function properly through the promotion of labor unions, the very forces that oppose the minimum wage most often oppose the very unions which wish to improve it. Unions have behaved

25   Ken Jacobs, Ian Perry and Jenifer MacGillvary, "The High Public Cost of Low Wages," *UC Berkeley Labor Center*, April 13, 2015

badly in the past and sometimes against workers' interests (and the history of American unions shows many deficiencies, which easily could fill another book by themselves); they can and should be, however, a necessary and powerfully beneficial force in defending the workers' interests.

> "It is much more difficult to judge one-self than to judge others."
>
> —Antoine de Saint-Exupéry
> *The Little Prince*

As aforementioned, reducing high welfare spending requires accepting increased pricing for the products sold by the companies paying minimum wages. Again, this is something that must be tackled in order to break through to a healthier market and stronger economy. The bottom line is that there can be no true free market if the government has to subsidize workers to compensate for their low wages.

The objections to a sustainable living minimum wage have been consistent since the concept was first introduced by President Roosevelt in 1933. Each was addressed and discredited through Franklin Roosevelt's statement on the National Industrial Recovery Act: "By living wages, I mean more than a bare subsistence level—I mean the wages of a decent living."[26] President Roosevelt's opinion is the same argument that is made today by minimum wage advocates.

---

[26] Franklin Roosevelt's Statement on the National Industrial Recovery Act June 16, 1933, cited in the New York Times, March 7, 2014

And what of the emotional toil of belonging to the lowest group of wage earners, regardless of the catalysts leading to this situation (perhaps lack of education or physical or emotional capacity, or perhaps influenced by one's age or the language barriers)? Being underpaid leaves people feeling unmotivated and undignified, and surely has an impact on job performance and, ultimately, customer service. Even something as simple as an employee's friendly smile makes a huge difference and has the power to attract and retain customers. Investing in the wellbeing of employees, in the most humane sense of the word, is a massive investment in and of itself.

Finally, standing in long lines for food stamps and other welfare benefits in crowded welfare offices is time-consuming. It takes away from precious time that could be used working and earning money. Hard-working people are being challenged and pushed to their limits.

The critical question remains: is the American market economy alive and well? I argue that the U.S. economy would collapse if it were not for the entitlement programs. Eliminating food stamps or rent assistance altogether without guaranteeing this group of people a minimum wage or subsidies would create chaos. Unable to pay their rent or their bills, working families would be driven to the streets. Homelessness would soar. Childhood malnutrition, mass starvation, and criminal activity would rise to record levels.

Is it okay for poor people to starve to death? *New York Times* columnist and 2008 Nobel laureate for Economics Paul Krugman wrote in May 2015 that "the haves" believe there are sufficient welfare programs available to "the have-nots," allowing them to lead a life of splendor.[27] The popular adage of "the harder you

---

[27] Paul Krugman, "The Insecure American," *The New York Times*, May 29,

work, the more you get" turns out to be an illusion. The government has not been successful in lowering the poverty rate over the decades, confirming that the current structure has failed. On the contrary, we are curtailing market forces, which may perhaps be one reason for the unresolved poverty issue. In my research, I have uncovered additional triggers. These are outlined in more detail below.

Corporate Subsidies Undermine the Market Economy

Wage subsidies are defined as the transfer of wealth from the taxpayer to the owners of companies employing subsidized workers. When the employer pays wages that are so low that employees need supplemental wage subsidies, it is implied that the real costs of adequate wages for the company are not being covered. Such a business is benefitting indirectly from government-funded wage subsidies. The actual cost of doing business is distorted. If such a company pays executive salaries or shows a profit, then, indirectly, the taxpayer is subsidizing that company. Robert Reich calls this money transfer an "upward redistribution."[28]

I agree that not every taxpayer is a customer of a fast-food restaurant, Walmart store, or any similar business. The theory of market economy asserts that consumers should pay for the products and services they use and not for those of their neighbors; wage subsidies are as well supporting exports from agriculture and other export industries. In the end, American

---

2015.

[28] Robert Reich, "The Rigging of the American Market," *Huffington Post*, November 1, 2015.

taxpayers are paying twice for the products they consume: once at the store and then through their tax dollars which fund the entitlement programs that supplement the low wages. Not only are labor costs not calculated properly in this equation, but the lower consumer price is an inaccurate depiction of the actual price being paid by the taxpaying consumer for a given project.

The Poor

Some people have fallen in a poverty trap, as noted in the prior sections of this book, for a variety of reasons. Some of them are characterized as having little or no education, something that inarguably does not help them climb up a corporate ladder or brainstorm for a different sort of breakthrough. Stuck in this trap, they rarely have enough cash or credit to buy everyday items of decent quality.

Savings made by purchasing cheap items—whether these are shoes or automobiles—are eaten up by the respective product's short lifespan or by costly repairs, and ultimately lesser quality leads to higher costs. The "working poor" are lured by consumerism just like everyone else. There are certain big-ticket items like TVs, cars, or furniture that they simply cannot afford, but sellers' profits depend on convincing people that they *can* afford (and need) such things. Rent-to-own are more than happy to accommodate this need at interest rates that would make a mobster blush. As illuminated in an article by Jeff Spross, "the American poor can't afford to drop a one-time payment of $1,500 on a sofa, but they can afford monthly installments of $110 that ultimately add up to over $4,500 for a sofa over time." Purchases made on installment plans result in the end-price being a multiple of the original price, due to compounded interest and other charges. Just so, poor folks opt for renting a motel room per week for less than the one-time deposit it takes to rent an apartment, which winds up costing far more over the long haul. [29] They enter into a vicious cycle where their social benefits may be used to pay for all of those repairs, charges, and compounded interest.

Access to banking services may be limited—sometimes literally, as many banks "don't see the point" in opening a branch in economically weak areas.[30] Many low income people do not have a bank account and have to use private institutions to cash checks carrying high charges. If they do have a bank account and do not manage their funds carefully, they are further penalized with overdraft fees. Many financial institutions require a minimum balance.

A personal savings account is supposed to provide an economic cushion, but this is not possible for someone who is on welfare. In the words of *AlterNet*'s Greta Christina: "Being poor is expensive."[31] She argues that poverty is a social issue, and that there are patterns—drawing statistics from the Urban Institute—that show that a poor person has a two in three chance to stay in that category for at least a year, a two in three chance to return to poverty within five years supposing they do "break out", and a two in three chance that their children will be poor as well.[32]

---

[29] Jeff Spross, "Want to end poverty in America? It's pretty simple," *The Week*, January 21, 2015. [The author refers to other publications treating the same processes.]

[30] Spross, *Ibid.*

[31] Greta Christina, "7 Things People Who Say They're 'Fiscally Conservative But Socially Liberal' Don't Understand,'" *AlterNet*, May 20, 2015.

[32] Signe-Mary McKernan, Caroline Ratcliffe, and Stephanie R. Cellini, "Transitioning In and Out of Poverty", *The Urban Institute*, September 1, 2009.

The battle against true poverty starts with learning how to handle money. Often people who are classified as poor have forgotten—or have never learned—how to handle money. Budget assistance for managing a limited weekly or monthly paycheck allows for a dignified life.

The U.S. the Welfare State

The U.S. Federal Budget of 2016 reveals that $916 billion, or 24% of the budget, is spent on the Federal Government's pension program.[33] Another 26%, or $1014 billion, is spent on healthcare, compared to the 16% ($605 billion) spent on national defense. This, combined with how 48% of the average American household budget is channeled towards pensions and healthcare, is infallible proof that we are a welfare nation.

The aforementioned budget details regarding Social Security are misleading. We know that the Social Security Trust Fund was "borrowed" by the government under the Reagan Administration. Hartman, in his book, quotes Greenspan, who was an adviser to President Reagan at the time, as saying: "Just borrow from the [Baby] Boomer's savings account—the money in the Social Security Trust Fund—and, because you are borrowing 'government money' to fund 'government expenditures,' you don't have to list it as part of the deficit. Much of the deficit will magically seem to disappear, and nobody will know what you did until thirty years in the future when the Boomers begin to retire in 2015."[34]

---

[33] Center on Budget and Policy Priorities (CBPP): "Policy Basics: Where Do Our Tax Dollars Go?" October 4, 2017.
http://www.cbpp.org/research/policy-basics-where-do-our-federal-tax-dollars-go.

As a social program, Social Security was brilliantly planned and implemented in 1937 to be completely self-sufficient and self-sustaining. The workers themselves paid for the program through a small payroll tax. Collectively, these worker's funds accumulated at a much greater rate than the pensions that were paid out to those who were retiring. Over the decades, the surplus increased, amounting to over $2.6 trillion by 2011.[35] But, in reality, the money wasn't there; the government was nearly forced to delay payments to millions of people. This led to a Social Security crisis during the summer of 2011. Technically, Social Security had $2.6 trillion at hand and was completely solvent—when in fact it didn't have a dime. The U.S. government has not paid back this "borrowed" money, and as a result, the Social Security began to lose its solvency.

Have we really forgotten that the trillions of dollars paid into Social Security by the baby boomers were borrowed and spent by the U.S. Government during the 1980s to cover the budget deficits created by the Reagan Administration? The missing funds are now showing up as part of the Federal budget under welfare spending—a misrepresentation of economic facts. The Social Security Trust Fund was not "government money," as Greenspan wrongly advised. He knew exactly that this transaction was unjustified and that, down the road, this would have huge consequences: what political arrogance! This "borrowing" transaction was invented to hide the budget deficit and to avoid a tax raise or to reduce expenditures. That money belonged to the baby boomer generation, who paid their contributions into their Social Security accounts to be released

---

[34] Thom Hartman, *Screwed, The Undeclared War Against the Middle Class*, San Francisco: BK Berrett-Koehler Publishers Inc., 2006, p. 165.
[35] Merril Matthews, "What Happened to the $2.6 Trillion Social Security Trust Fund?", *Forbes*, July 13, 2011.

just about today. Today's Social Security payments are not entitlement subsidies, as is often declared; today, the taxpayers simply reimburse this money to the baby boomers. Thus, 24% of the budget is actually the repayment of a loan from the baby boomers.

The fact that half of the Federal budget is used to supplement social programs has a bigger impact on the social structure than many want to acknowledge. Poverty is a social construct. The low minimum wage creates structural poverty and, as a result, keeps welfare recipients trapped in a vicious cycle. The Republican Party in Congress despises the "entitlement society" (as they call the poor) and suggests eliminating welfare programs altogether. Americans fear that the U.S. will become a welfare state following the model of European countries—yet, America cannot *become* a welfare state because it already *is* a welfare state. All Federal social programs are funded by the American taxpayer, including Social Security, as explained above. Because of this economic thinking error, Social Security benefits today are paid out of the Federal budget instead of the Social Security fund.

With an income below the poverty level, individuals and families can apply for food stamps and are entitled to Medicaid. A family earning the minimum wage with only one source of income is entitled to other social programs as well. Depending on how much total income the family earns, it can apply for direct payments such as the Temporary Assistance to Needy Families program.[36] Based on their low income, they are tax-exempt on the Federal, state, and local level. Health insurance contributions are supplemented by the government as well.

---

[36] Wikipedia: "Welfare, USA." [consulted January 24, 2016]. https://en.wikipedia.org/wiki/Welfare#United_States.

American Thinker reporter Rick Moran states that the U.S. has 200 social programs, and 23% of the nation's population uses the three largest programs: Temporary Assistance to Needy Families, Supplemental Security Income, and the Supplemental Nutrition Assistance Program (commonly known as food stamps).[37] Singles below the poverty line are supported with payments up to $17,000, and families up to $50,000, annually.[38] Moran reports that welfare benefits have strongly increased since the beginning of the War on Poverty in 1969.

Good health is not guaranteed. We can contribute to it by eating healthy food and exercising and taking good care of our bodies. If we need to consult a doctor or undergo surgery, we want to have funds available; hence, planning for the future includes planning for medical emergencies. Health insurance is the most efficient way to pay for such expenditures, so we pay life-long monthly premiums to our health-insurance companies with the promise that they will later cover our expenses. Economically justified, every one of us is responsible for the cost of our healthcare, and we should not rely on the average taxpayer. The same principles apply when you plan for retirement. You commit to paying into your Social Security account and company pension fund, and that provides the foundation for your Golden Age. You fund your future lifestyle.

Healthy young people generally do not worry about illness and pensions—it is, however, solidarity that makes the system work. The system is most effective when everybody pays a fair share over a long period of time. The more people pay into the system, the lower the contributions are. Only mandatory

[37] Rick Moran, "Percentage of Americans on welfare hits record levels," *American Thinker,* July 9, 2014.
[38] Peter Ferrara, "'Welfare State' Doesn't Adequately Describe How Much America's Poor Control Your Wallet," *Forbes,* June 23, 2013.

government rules can realize this model: legislation sets the goal; private companies or non-profit organizations execute the plan. Mandatory healthcare and a mandatory retirement plan would allow most people to master their financial life. Moreover, a good social benefit structure would relieve the taxpayer of having to support the high welfare cost of those who are not insured.

Instead, let us acknowledge that America is a fully developed welfare state: the taxpayer is taking care of its needy citizens in the form of welfare programs. Permanent underpay and the lack of social benefits are the leading causes of poverty. Underpay leads to induced poverty and subsequent horrendous welfare spending, a consequence that goes unnoticed—or is, at least, unattended—by mainstream politics.

In a perfect world, people have food, housing, clothes, education, good health, and savings for retirement. To reach this high standard of living, each individual has to work hard and work smart. He or she must spend earnings wisely. A small amount of the funds has to be saved for the future. Careful financial planning is a lifetime challenge and should be a continuous goal.

Every individual is responsible for his health and his retirement. Ideally, all Americans do make enough income during their working years to meet their healthcare needs and save for retirement. I suggest legislation to guide and support the constituents to reach these goals. Before 1980, the deregulation of health care, we had a functional and efficient system.

Part 2: Institutional Poverty Traps

As mentioned before, I say poverty in this country is created by institutional mechanisms and sustained and kept in place, possibly even unconsciously. The distinction "poverty traps" I created to unveil the reasons for continued and unresolved poverty issues in this country. Poverty exists in every society, and it becomes a critical issue when persistent, and particularly when paired with low-wage conditions and poor healthcare coverage.

Can we avoid poverty?

The welfare of citizens and their protection is the responsibility of a democratic government, in other words, the legislators have to orchestrate economic and political development to secure the safety and wellbeing, and a basic life style for all American citizens, including the needy. We elect political officials to manage the country and serve its citizens.

Half of the Federal budget is spent on social programs. While this is a noble act it does not resolve the current persistent level of poverty. Here is my analysis.

Low Minimum Wage

As stated in the chapter "Poverty as a Structural Problem", people who work for the minimum wage cannot live a decent life no matter how hard they work. Part of the middle class, as well as low-income households, fall into this category. The so-called "working poor" do not make enough money to put food on the table, let alone support a family, based solely on the current Federal minimum wage of $7.25 per hour.[39] Because they can barely survive, low-income wage earners depend on receiving help from third parties. Whether or not the help comes from official sources (such as counties, states, or the Federal Government) or from volunteer organizations (such as churches and non-profit organizations) is irrelevant: poverty is widespread.

The minimum wage must be defined such that it is possible for workers to make a living from the wages they earn. To be clear: the government-regulated minimum wage has a lot to do with poverty today.

Part-time Employment

Prior to the 1970s, most jobs were well-paid full-time jobs, while part-time work was more widely considered a teenager's supplemental income. The women's movement created a huge shift in the job market place. While the opening of the workplace for woman was a huge achievement, it doubled at the same time

---

[39] The minimum wage set by the Federal Government is at $7.25 per hour (since July 2009). Performing work in connection with federal contracts is paid $10.35 effective January 2018. In some states, it may be higher.

the number of workers overnight without respectively doubling the jobs. To compensate for this, many employers dropped the full-time positions and instead filled these same hours with multiple part-time employees. "Part-time" workers are those who work 35 hours or less per week. Along with the reduction in full-time workers, companies found that they could get away with lowering wages; it was simply a matter of supply and demand.

This transition encouraged men and women to have equal opportunity for these jobs, but morphed them into low-paying, part-time positions. A lot of this had to do with the doubling of the workforce and stiffer competition for each job. This trend eventually leveled off and the number of part-time workers remained rather static up until the Great Recession of 2007.

Prior to the recession, the number of part-time workers stood at 5.8 million. As the economy recovered, there was minimal effort to create full-time work; that figure skyrocketed by another 2.8 million.[40] The actual percentage of part-time workers still comprises a minority of the work force.

Although part-time jobs help decrease unemployment, it can lead to poverty and I consider part-time employment a potential poverty trap. Here are the facts; part-time employees are excluded from contributing to social programs such as pension plans, and health and accident insurance. Part time employees carry this financial burden. In contrast, a full-time employee reaps the benefits of healthcare, a pension plan, paid time-off and vacations. The part-timer receives wages without benefits other than the Social Security.

---

[40] Catherine Rampell, "The Rise of Part-Time Work," *The New York Times*, March 8, 2013.

According to Chantal Panozzo, an American citizen, who lived and worked part time in Switzerland for ten years, contribution to social programs, including the pension plan, is mandatory for part time as well as full time employees. When Panozzo switched from full- to part-time employment, she was not excluded from participating in the system of social benefits.

She was able to choose to work either five half-days or two-and-a-half full days a week to fulfill on her weekly workload. This flexibility allowed her, as a working mother, to maintain her security, and contribute to her pension plan as part-time worker.

"The Swiss have a culture of professional part-time work," she explains, "and as a result, part-time jobs include every benefit of a full-time job, including vacation time and payment into two Swiss pension systems. Salaries for part-time work are set as a percentage of a professional full-time salary because unlike the United States, part-time jobs are not viewed as necessarily unskilled jobs with their attendant lower pay."[41]

Returning to the U.S. in 2013, she wrote that working conditions seemed backward and absurd in contrast. She realized that she could only participate and contribute to social programs if she worked full-time and could enjoy none of the benefits that she used to as a part-time employee. Giving up full-time employment meant a return to hourly wages, with the only deduction being Social Security.

The logic of only including full-time employees in the participation of social programs such as healthcare and retirement plan is a missed opportunity for part-time employees.

There is no reason that makes economic sense to exclude part-time employees from social deductions and pension plans. Every employee should pay contributions to the system of Social

---

[41]   Panozzo, *Ibid.*

Security and a pension fund, and finally profit from two annuities when becoming a senior.

As Panozzo reported in her 2015 article for *Vox.com*, part-time employees make up 5.5% of the workforce in Nebraska, and 16% of employees are part-time in California, Arizona, and Nevada.[42]

The libertarian and conservative intention to create opportunities for more part-time workers has spread to education. Author and political activist Noam Chomsky wrote in a 2014 article about a 1997 Senate hearing in which Alan Greenspan, then Chairman of the Federal Reserve, said that economic success is based on "greater worker insecurity."[43] Greenspan called job insecurity "healthy" for society, explaining that job scarcity would discourage the employed from asking for a raise, force them to refrain from instigating a strike, and cause them to "gladly and passively" obey their employers.

Greenspan showed neither empathy for the middle-class employee nor any interest at all in improving job conditions. In his view, there are rich people and poor people, and there is nothing we can do about it; it is just a part of human development. Chomsky additionally reported that, at the time, Greenspan's statement was ignored by the public, who today surely feel the full economic impact of 20% of the population living below the Federal poverty line. Greenspan, a key player in

---

[42]   Chantal Panozzo, "Living in Switzerland ruined me for America and its lousy work culture," *vox.com*, July 21, 2015, http ://www.vox.com/2015/7/21/8974435/switzerland-work-life-balance

[43]   Noam Chomsky, "How America's Great University System is Being Destroyed. Faculty are increasingly hired on the Walmart model as temps," *AlterNet*, February 28, 2014. [Refers to the *The Federal Reserve Board Protocol*, "Testimony of Chairman Alan Greenspan," February 26, 1997].

American economic policy, completely misjudged the impact of the statement, or did not care.

The Gig Economy

Young companies, such as Uber and Lyft, provide innovative service jobs for on-demand taxi rides and consumer goods delivery, respectively, which allow better use of existing capacity in the transportation industry.[44] These services are mainly directed towards individuals or businesses in the private sector who wish to transport themselves or consumer goods from one place to another. Uber and Lyft act as agents or brokers between the supplier of transport services and the demand for a ride.[45] The higher degree of capacity utilization is economically efficient; hence, these startups are instantly valued at billions of dollars, while their job-brokering activities give rise to a mixture of admiration and dislike.

Brokering companies for other fields of work are already flourishing; examples include Fiverr and Upwork (online agencies for jobs in software coding, advertising, the graphic arts, marketing, and more) as well as Homejoy (a platform for housecleaning jobs). The jobs themselves are small and clearly structured; however, the status of the contractor is not clear. Contractors are not employees of the intermediary companies. They are now being called "independent contractors" who get paid for short-term contracts. I would call these jobs "day labor": short work periods with immediate cash payment.

---

[44] www.uber.com and www.lyft.com are well-known agencies in the transportation sector.

[45] Katy Steinmetz, "Is the on-demand economy taking workers for a ride?" *Time Magazine,* August 3, 2015.

Independent contracting is becoming an increasingly larger portion of the workforce in the 21st century. Although it is difficult to fully calculate the number of part-time workers today (independent contractors, self-employed workers, and contingent workers), it is estimated at around 35% of the workforce in 2010 and has certainly increased since.[46] Technology has expedited this growth and today there are hundreds of sites soliciting the independent contractor in industries ranging from writing and teaching to computer programming and corporate law.

Major issues remain in question. Issues of liability and responsibility remain largely unresolved. What should customers expect if there is a misfortune or setback? Are these "independent contractors" ready to assume liability in case of an accident? Are the self-contractors thinking about saving for the future, are they paying into social security and pension funds?

If this kind of "independent contract" work lasts only for a limited time and attracts mostly young people, then it can be compared to a part-time student job. Working as a "day-laborer" may work for a short period of time, but what if these day-laborers work under these conditions for years? Employees have many fringe benefits paid by the employer like healthcare, pension funds, and insurance that covers accidents.

This new "independent contractor" concept intensifies the pressure on other local companies; existing workers' contracts with employment benefits are now compared to work without benefits. In fact, the day-laborer job concept is a negative spiral leading to poverty; the supposedly good pay rate does not include any benefits and does not help build pensions and

---

[46] Elaine Pofeldt, "Shocker: 40% of Workers Now Have 'Contingent' Jobs, Says U.S. Government", *Forbes,* May 25, 2015 and "Freelancers Now Make Up 35% Of U.S. Workforce", *Forbes,* October 6, 2016

retirement savings. Is the Libertarian concept of dividing mankind into classifications of the very rich and very poor on its way to triumph? Is this goal a world without social benefits? The digital world opens opportunities to make fast money. The biggest question is: what is the effect on our society? Libertarian politics likes to lean on private business activity, except without the help of any government services.

Healthcare

We cannot talk about healthcare reform without first considering its history. Up until the 1960s, healthcare reform really wasn't much of an issue.[47] Healthcare was largely a publicly controlled service, freely allowing independent doctors to put up signs advertising their services without being attached to corporations. For the most part, hospitals were run by counties, churches, or municipalities.

In 1965, however, President Lyndon Johnson signed the Social Security Amendments which established Medicare and Medicaid to provide insurance for the poor and elderly as part of his sweeping social reform plan. Medicaid is a health insurance program that assists families and individuals with low income. It is a joint federal and state program, with the federal government funding up to 50% (on average) of the cost of a state's Medicaid program. More affluent states receive less funding than their less affluent counterparts; to be fair in that respect, there's actually a specific Medicaid program for each individual state.

---

[47] "PBS -Healthcare Crisis, Healthcare Timeline," www.pbs.org/healthcarecrisis/history.htm.

Medicare is available only to people who are 65 years old and older, as well as to people with permanent disabilities, and it is available to these citizens regardless of income. This insurance covers between 60%-85% of costs; the rest is paid by the patient or is covered by an additional insurance. Medicare as a health insurance is funded by Social Security contributions (payroll taxes). The expenditures are higher than the contributions so a large part of the remaining portion is paid out of the U.S. Treasury.

Throughout the 1970s, corporations were first beginning to discern the profit margin involved with healthcare. This was only further encouraged when President Richard Nixon introduced the concept of health maintenance organizations (or, as they became popularly known, HMOs).[48] Interestingly, Nixon reintroduced the idea of a national health insurance program which would provide a form of universal healthcare for all Americans. It was not the Medicare for all citizens that Senator Ted Kennedy was advocating for at the time, but it was a small step in the direction of a general health insurance system.[49]

Nixon explained the situation of millions of American citizens during a special message to Congress on February 6th, 1974: "First, even though more Americans carry health insurance than ever before, the 25 million Americans who remain uninsured often need it the most and are most unlikely to obtain it. They include many who work in seasonal or transient occupations, high-risk cases, and those who are ineligible for Medicaid despite low incomes." Ironically, the number of uninsured Americans, declared by Nixon back in 1974, is still the same today.

---

[48] Jeff Griffin, "The History of Healthcare in America," *JP Griffin Group*, March 7, 2017.

[49] "Nixon's Plan For Health Reform, His Own Words," *KHN Kaiser Health News*, September 03, 2009.

Corporations really began wrestling for control over healthcare thanks to the massive deregulation initiated by President Ronald Reagan in the 1980s. It was during this period that healthcare services became consolidated and came under the control of corporations. This decade saw as well the demise of the independent small-town doctor; in order to have hospital rights, such doctors were suddenly forced to become part of a corporate organization. This healthcare consolidation continued throughout the 1990s under President Clinton.

According to the Henry J. Kaiser Foundation, more than 55 million individuals received health coverage through Medicare in 2016 and Federal budget costs were $588 billion—which comes out to about 15% of the total federal budget.[50] Higher healthcare costs, the increased number of Baby Boomers entering retirement, and a higher life expectancy all resulted in the Federal budget strain. This became a negative trend toward a higher Federal deficit.

The logic of Medicare—that medical services for those over the age of 65 are paid for by the Federal government—gives the impression that Americans are always healthy before they reach that milestone age and have no need for coverage in the event of illness. This is certainly not realistic. While President Johnson's 1965 Medicare Bill was an excellent start to healthcare coverage, it excluded people who were younger than 65 years old. This changed in January 2014 when healthcare insurance became mandatory for all.

---

[50] The Henry J. Kaiser Family Foundation, "The Total Number of Medicare Beneficiaries", Time Frame 2015. And: Juliette Cubanski and Tricia Neumann, "The Facts on Medicare Spending and Financing", *The Henry J. Kaiser Family Foundation*, July 18, 2017.

High Cost of Health Care

The U.S. healthcare system is known throughout the world as unique. A 2007 survey by the Commonwealth Fund, which compared healthcare systems in the U.S., Australia, New Zealand, the UK, Germany, and Canada, found that the American system is the most expensive on the planet.[51] The survey showed that America was the only country without mandatory health insurance coverage and that its patients had more insurance payments denied, more disputes with insurance companies, and more out-of-pocket expenses than did residents of other countries.

A 2010 survey written up in *Health Affairs Magazine* found "significant differences in access, cost burdens, and problems with health insurance that are associated with design. U.S. adults were the most likely to incur high medical expenses, even when insured, and had to spend time on insurance paperwork and disputes or to have payments denied."[52]

In the January 9/2016 issue of *The Nation,* writer Robert Sherrill lists reasons for these enormous costs; high salaries of insurance company CEOs, the preference of brand-name medication over generic medication, high charges for aspirin or paper tissues in hospitals, greater frequency of expensive operations, medical specialists' salaries, expensive malpractice insurance, and much more.[53] Additionally, insurance company

---

[51] "Mirror, Mirror on the Wall: An International Update on the Comparative Performance of American Health Care," *The Commonwealth Fund,* May 15, 2007 and updates to June 16, 2014.

[52] Cathy Schoen et al. "How Health Insurance Design Affects Access To Care And Costs, By Income, In Eleven Countries," *Health Affairs* (Health Aff 10.1377/hlthaff.2010.0862, 2010).

[53] Robert Sherrill, "The Most Expensive Health Care System in the World," *The Donella Meadows Archive, Voice of a Global Citizen,* Sustainability

shareholders expect a huge profit. In their entirety, wrote Tara Culp-Ressler in a 2014 *ThinkProgress* article, these facts are an American phenomenon and are the foundation of exceedingly high health costs.[54]

How are benefits calculated? Steven Brill of *Time Magazine* cites in his article "Bitter Pill, Why Medical Bills Are Killing Us", that the codes and price list of services (called a "charge master") are created by hospitals and doctors who are at a very high level.[55] If I were to show up at the hospital to be treated, would I be seeing prices that are more appropriate for a rich Saudi prince? Will be treatment be fairly priced? The price approaches differ from hospital to hospital and are not logical. The most extreme example cited by Brill is a daylong treatment that was billed at $87,000.

These extra and often exorbitant costs are not the result of doctors or nurses who actually provide the care; rather, they are the brainchild of corporate hospitals. The unchecked freedom to invoice services—with absurd costs such as charging $70 for a box of tissues—distorts the cost/performance ratio. Unfortunately, the patient is completely at the mercy of the corporate hospitals when it comes to such charges.

Brill compares these prices with those paid for by Medicare. The price differences are enormous. The level of Medicare prices is usually a fraction of those offered by charge master rates; therefore it is very important to have health insurance. Only insurance coverage guarantees that American residents will pay moderate prices, as they must have been negotiated.

Institute, (Hartland, VT: no date).
[54] Tara Culp-Ressler, "The U.S. Has The Most Expensive And Least Effective Health Care In The Developed World," *ThinkProgress,* June 16, 2014.
[55] Steven Brill, „Bitter Pill, Why Medical Bills Are Killing Us", Special report, *Time Magazine*, March 4, 2013.

With mandatory healthcare coverage, the prices applied are lower compared to those of the free market. With mandatory healthcare, the rates of hospitals, medical services, and laboratories must come down and will eventually coincide with the level of Medicare rates.

Why are the American healthcare-costs the highest in the world? A study showed surprising details. As Margot Sanger-Katz reports in an article for *The New York Time/The Upshot*, patients in the U.S. do not go more often to hospitals or doctor's practice, they have not more and complicated treatments and the administrative costs are comparable to other countries. The big difference is that American patients pay "substantially higher prices for medical services, including hospitalization, doctors' visits and prescription drugs."[56]

It is because healthcare is a profit driven business enterprise and not a human right. The healthcare profit chain extends right on down to the insurance companies who experienced record profits again during 2017. The insurance company Aetna reported to the Securities and Exchange Commission a compensation of $27.9 million to their CEO Mark Bertolini in 2015...[57]

If American healthcare were a nation, it would be the world's fifth largest economy at three trillion dollars. In fact, according to *Consumer Reports,* "person per person, health care in the U.S. costs about twice as much as it does in the rest of the developed

---

[56] Margot Sanger-Katz, "Why Is U.S. Health Care So Expensive? Some of the Reasons You've Heard Turn Out to Be Myths," *The New York Times/The Upshot,* March 13, 2018. The report is based on a study published by *The Journal of the American Medical Association.*

[57] https://www.consumeraffairs.com/news/health-insurance-industry-rakes-in-billions-while-blaming-obamacare-for-losses-110116.html

world."[58] All of this adds up to higher premiums for those who are insured and insurmountable debt for those who are not.

The healthcare market is on the move. The latest proposal for a high quality and affordable care insurance company comes from the trio Warren Buffet of Berkshire Hathaway, Jeff Bezos of Amazon, and Jamie Dimon of JP Morgan Chase.[59] The goal is to found a new company which will be independent and "free from profit-making incentives and constraints." The intention will be to contract doctors and hospitals directly for "better deals." This is a private initiative with good goals. Nevertheless, it is urgent for the United States to pass legislation for a decent healthcare system.

Admittedly, healthcare costs are increasing worldwide. The health insurance system suffers mainly because stakeholders do not show any interest in producing cheaper services or products. Patients demand the best doctors and hospitals, who, in turn, charge higher prices because of their status. Pharmaceutical conglomerates offer expensive research results in the form of new medications, and insurance companies act as intermediaries for their services.

---

[58] "Why is health care so expensive? Why it's so high, how it affects your wallet—and yes, what you can do about it," *Consumer Reports*, September 2014.

[59] Tim Murphy, "Amazon, Buffet, JPMorgan join forces on health care", *The Associated Press/The Aspen Times,* January 31, 2018.

Non-Mandatory Health Insurance

During his second year in office, President Barack Obama made good on his 2008 campaign promise to introduce mandatory health insurance and signed the Patient Protection and Affordable Care Act of 2010 into law. Both the House and Senate, with Democratic majorities, agreed to the plan. As of January 2014, residents of the United States are required to have health insurance or pay a penalty. President Obama's reasoning was to prevent people from waiting until they got sick to buy health insurance. Under this new law, close to 30 million Americans could benefit from insurance coverage. Pre-existing conditions were no longer allowed to exclude patients from coverage. There has been a long list of pros and cons to what has since been nicknamed "Obamacare".

In my opinion, with millions more insured and paying premiums, the individual health insurance premium ought to decrease. The so-called "good risks" in this equation (the young and healthy citizens) will pay their premiums so that when they are in need of insurance benefits, they can fall back on their coverage. Because younger people require fewer medical services than people in midlife, the contributions will balance the cost. This is an ideal health insurance model which thrives on a mentality of solidarity. The act of solidarity provides a safety net for all in case of an emergency.

Mandatory health insurance means that every resident in this country is committed to paying a monthly contribution for the benefit of the larger society, which includes said respective resident. The monthly insurance premium guarantees that health expenses are covered and that the insurance is the guarantor of limited expenses in case of need. In theory, the sum of monthly contributions goes into a fund which will pay for medical and hospital costs; everyone, across all age groups, contributes to the fund. Everyone, across all age groups, is entitled to receive help from it as well.

A great advantage of mandatory healthcare is that patients must pay negotiated prices. Insurance companies, including Medicare, negotiate the prices with hospitals and medical services. Whoever is covered by a healthcare plan pays a pre-determined price (for visits to the hospital or doctor) that is agreed upon by the insurance company. Since all residents must now have healthcare insurance, these prices will have to be paid, either in-full or partially, by insurance companies. The poverty trap described above will become a thing of the past.

In part, this would require a fundamental shift from a "me" society to a "we" society. The cost of insurance will now become a collective investment in our nation's wellbeing. The bottom line is: Americans must care for Americans. The United States is a political entity which must feel responsible for its constituents.

The ideal system of healthcare contributions is a single-payer system; every American pays his part to his or her healthcare costs. This might be comparable to the car insurance model where, in such a case, every single person or a family who drives must legally have insurance.

The mandatory insurance rule decreased the number of uninsured residents from 48 million to about 28 million as of 2016.[60] Obamacare was aimed at about 15% of the population.

Employees of large companies as well as government and state authorities, on the contrary, appear to be protected and

---

[60]   Nicholas Bakalar, "Nearly 20 Million Have Gained Health Insurance Since 2010", *The New York Times*, May 22, 2017.

well cared for with their existing health insurance and pension plans.

Mandatory health insurance is highly contested in the U.S. This is exemplified in how practically all respective Federal government regulations are met with suspicion and treated with utmost skepticism. The introduction of Obamacare was no exception. This Act is often refuted on principle and has become a political battle. The Constitution of the United States is very strict when it comes to protecting its citizens from its own government. In 2012, the U.S. Supreme Court in the case National Federation of Independent Business v. Sebelius ruled in favor of the constitutionality of the ACA.

The ACA of 2010 is heading in the right direction, toward eliminating the Healthcare Poverty Trap. Brokered prices are paid by the healthcare insurers and not by uninsured patients who are financially overtaxed. The best results are achieved by a mandatory health insurance system. Citizens who purchase health insurance and pay the monthly rates will be protected from financial disaster in the case of major illness or costly surgeries.

Whoever cries "Repeal Obamacare!" is in fact for high social spending, and ultimately for maintaining or even increasing current tax levels. Repealing Obamacare is clearly the wrong way to reduce poverty and social spending. I am not saying that the ACA is an ideal solution, but it has the potential to unburden the Federal household with mandatory health insurance that covers each citizen's lifetime.

Are we switching from Obamacare to Trumpcare? To this day it is the goal of the Republican Party to repeal Obamacare. Fortunately or unfortunately, this party has not been able to create an attractive alternative since 2010 when Obamacare was invented. The Trump administration changed important details of Obamacare in October 2017, such as scrapping federal subsidies and enabling access to cheaper and skimpier insurance.[61] What will be the long-term effects? Experts do not know.

Lack of Retirement Plans

The U.S. pension plan model was designed on the "Three-Legged Stool" principle. The three legs are Social Security (the Federal pension plan), company pension-plan benefits, and private savings, all of which should collectively make retirement possible. Today, only payments into the Federal pension plan (Social Security) are mandatory in America; fewer and fewer Americans benefit from company pension plans. In fact, according to one study, only 20% of employees receive pensions today, down by half since 1990.[62]

Employees in the public sector receive 92% of their salary from their pension at retirement; those in the private sector get significantly less. Larger companies offer managed pension plans, whereas smaller companies prefer individual 401K accounts. A 401K account is, to be honest nothing more than a savings account, but the employee owns and controls these assets. These savings are fiscally preferred in the name of the employee.

Pension funds are professionally managed assets for retirement. The usual rules guarantee the insured, after retirement, a lifetime payout of a monthly sum based on savings

[61] Jessica Glenza, "Dismantling Obamacare: what has Trump done and who will it affect?", *The Guardian*, October 13, 2017.
[62] Jason DeRusha, "Good Question: How Many Of Us Still Get A Pension?" *CBS Local Minnesota*, October 17, 2012.

accrued during years spent in the workforce. Technically, pension fund assets must be kept off the company balance sheet and placed in a separate fund. The pension fund must have its own account for each insured person and has to send him an account statement every year. Corporations very often viewed these pensions as general available cash-on-hand. Pension fund savings listed in the balance sheet of a company, however, are lost in a case of bankruptcy.

Monthly contributions to a mandatory pension fund would reduce welfare spending down the road. In successful models, the employer pays an equal share into the fund, so that, after 40 years of funds accrued with interest, the retiree can look forward to a dignified retirement. However, pensions and their management cannot be left to the individual. Pension-fund institutions have the objective and obligation to provide secure payment at retirement. This requires highly professional and qualified people.

Some people believe that paying into social programs is a restriction of their personal freedom; they resist government regulations. Interestingly, opponents to social laws judge and despise the needy and wonder why so many elderly citizens are asking for support. Because many citizens do not or are unable to make sufficient provisions for their retirement during their productive years, they often end up in poverty during their "Golden Years" and are dependent on taxpayer support. This has resulted in citizens who are over 65 years old experiencing an extraordinary poverty rate of over 45%; a recent analysis from the Kaiser Foundation revealed that close to half of senior citizens had incomes below *twice* the Supplemental Poverty Measure threshold; the SPM differs in that it takes into account in-kind benefits (food stamps), liabilities (taxes), out-of-pocket medical spending, and so forth.[63]

Sadly, the "Three-Legged Stool" principle seems to have remained a mere theoretical concept.

In reality, the majority of Americans are ill-prepared for retirement—and the topic of retirement planning is not on the U.S. political agenda. The Federal pension plan, Social Security, is the most important source of income during retirement for many people in the middle class and lowest income brackets. The security blanket for the average American is stretched thin. A study by the Federal Reserve, according to American economist Paul Krugman, claims that 47% of citizens cannot afford an unexpected expense of $400.[64] Krugman worries that the political elite will not make adequate decisions because of a lack of understanding of, and empathy for, the lower-income population.

---

[63] Juliette Cubanski, Giselle Casillas and Anthony Damico, "Poverty Among Seniors: An Updated Analysis of National and State Level Poverty Rates Under the Official and Supplemental Poverty Measures," *The Henry J. Kaiser Family Foundation*, June 10, 2015.

[64] Paul Krugman, "Report on the Economic Well-Being on U.S. Households in 2014," *Board of Governors of the Federal Reserve System*, May 2015.

Part 3:
American Economy

The Government's Income and the Broken Tax Code

When examining the Federal Government's financial problems, it is important to take a closer look at funding. Tax laws must be changed or fundamentally improved in order to create a balanced budget. It is a fact that the super-rich in America pay fewer taxes by taking advantage of current tax legislation. Officially, the tax code is progressive and it is applicable to every citizen. There are plenty of opportunities to halve the tax burden if you are wealthy. According to *The Washington Post*, 2012 Republican presidential candidate Mitt Romney was taxed 16% on his income of $20 million, while former Speaker of the House Newt Gingrich, with an income of $3 million, paid a Federal income tax bill of 30%.[65]

This is not coincidental. In 1981, President Reagan had Congress change the tax laws so that the highest income earners would pay fewer taxes. The rationale was that the richest Americans require a tax reduction so that this portion of their wealth—that would otherwise be taken through taxation—is

---

[65]   Lori Montgomery, Jia Lynn Yang and Philip Rucker, "Mitt Romney releases tax returns", *The Washington Post*, January 24, 2012.

instead invested by these wealthy citizens in the country. This is known as *supply-side economics*. This policy was a turning point in American economic history.[66] A lower tax burden for individuals and businesses was the beginning of a development of low productivity in manufacturing (see below), a growing gap between the rich and poor, and a catalyst for loopholes and strange ambiguities when it came to the taxes of the very rich and the corporations.

Since the 1960s, budget expenditures were higher than the tax revenues; this eventually resulted in today's huge Federal dept. In Congress, Democrats were in favor of ongoing changes of taxation, while Republicans wanted to delay any changes until there could be a discussion of the entire tax law.

The Republican Party kept the word and renewed the tax legislation from the ground up in December 2017; this has since set in motion a number of changes which will impact many well-known principles for individual and corporate taxation. These changes follow, to a certain degree, the theory of the flat tax system.[67] Several of the changes will include: an elimination of double taxation for individuals when living abroad, lowered income tax rates, and adjustments to some standard deductions. These new rules will expire in 2025. Although this reformed legislation is meant to help certain categories of people, it will

---

[66] Supply-side economics proposes that tax decreases may lead to economic growth. Historical data, however, shows no significant correlation between lower top marginal tax rates and Gross Domestic Product (GDP) growth rate.

[67] "A flat tax (short for flat tax rate) is a tax system with a constant marginal rate, usually applied to individual or corporate income. A true flat tax would be a proportional tax, but implementations are often progressive and sometimes regressive depending on deductions and exemptions in the tax base." Wikipedia

overall have a very negative impact on the national debt, which will continue to scale for many years.

American corporations doing business internationally are constantly looking for tax advantages. They have, as of this point in time, no scruples about shifting their activities and services abroad in order to reduce taxes. When the official maximum corporate income tax rate was 35% (at least until 2017), over 300 of the largest companies on the *Fortune 500* list therefore arranged to incur their profits abroad.[68] It is customary for American companies to transfer patents, brands, or company names (intellectual properties) to countries with low tax rates, especially Ireland, the United Kingdom, Bermuda, the Netherlands, Switzerland, and Singapore, or to register them in those countries first.[69] American corporations report earnings from those countries to the IRS. As long as the profits are not transferred to the U.S., they cannot be taxed by the U.S.

American pharmaceutical and electronics companies expect their patents and intellectual properties to be protected by U.S. legislation, yet they take the liberty to transfer production to other countries so save on taxes in America. On one hand this is an exploitation of government services and on the other hand it is an avoidance of obligations.

Richard Rubin wrote for *Bloomberg Business* in 2015 that Gilead Sciences Inc. first registered the trademark for its bestselling drug *Sovaldi* in Ireland. This was before the American Food and Drug Administration approved the product for the U.S. market.[70] Ireland's low tax rate of 12.5% on corporate profits undoubtedly tipped the balance in favor of registering abroad.

---

68   List of the 500 largest American companies by total revenue, *Fortune Magazine, published every year.*
69   Richard Rubin, "U.S. Companies Are Stashing $2.1 Trillion Overseas to Avoid Taxes," *Bloomberg Business*, March 4, 2015.

Companies with intellectual properties have an advantage over physical manufacturing plants and the financial sector. According to Rubin, it is not surprising that Microsoft, Apple, Google, and Pfizer legally leave their profits abroad to avoid the U.S. tax rate of 35% in place until 2017.[71] As a result, other countries are eager to set favorable tax rates and advantageous parameters, both to keep their own companies within their borders and to attract American companies. As Rubin notes: "the response of U.S.-based companies over the past few years has been consistent: book profits offshore and leave them there."[72]

Because of those former U.S. tax laws, American corporations have very high liquidity—abroad. *Business Insider* reports that, in 2014, American corporations kept $1.95 trillion overseas.[73] In 2005, the American Jobs Creation Act had reduced tax rates in an attempt to entice corporations to bring that money back home. Unfortunately, it was unsuccessful.[74] Hopefully the new tax code of December 2017 will animate the American corporations to transfer their immense liquidity from abroad to the States, where it would be taxed at a one-time repatriation tax of 15%.

The U.S. Federal business tax rate was ranked among the highest worldwide. The current tax rate of 20% makes the U.S. more competitive in this respect, but there are no guarantees on how companies will respond. Corporations can always claim depreciation, value adjustments, or negative earnings reports. All taxpayers, including individuals as well as businesses, are allowed to use the tax code to optimize their tax burden. Some

---

[70] Richard Rubin, *ante.*
[71] Richard Rubin, *ante.*
[72] Richard Rubin, *ante.*
[73] Akin Oyedele, "Here is the ridiculous amount of cash US companies are stashing overseas," *Business Insider*, March 17, 2015.
[74] Oyedele, *Ibid.*

current tax laws, however, are ridiculously unfair and lean heavily in favor of the very rich and the big corporations. Lobbying ensued in the influencing of tax legislation with the effect of extremely undemocratic and unjustified results—all technically legal but clearly unfair.

American corporations can transfer their tax domicile out of the country by purchasing a small company in Canada or Europe. That small company is then turned into the acquiring or parent company; in other words, the actual purchasing company becomes the acquiree. In this way, the original company has been transformed into a foreign, non-U.S. entity, and will use its new identity as its tax base.

Such a transformation is called a "corporate inversion," for which the rules and regulations were tightened in 2014 and 2015. Regulatory attention was directed at the identity of companies that wish to carry out inversions. Additionally, companies were classified as American if 80% or more of their shareholders are American. Following this, however, the Obama administration proposed a reduction of the percentage of American shareholder ownership to 50%, which would bring about a tax liability under IRS rules and increase the cost of inversion.

A new law passed under Obama, introduced a tax liability if tax avoidance was the main reason for company takeovers. Inversion financing is often done with bank loans. Under the Obama law, bridge financing of this nature could then be classified and taxed as a dividend. Overall, the incentives and loopholes of old U.S. tax laws have yielded conspicuously distorted results. Exxon, for example, is one of the largest oil and gas companies, with 80% of its activities in the U.S. Interestingly it files only 17% of its business volume as generated within the U.S. and, therefore, only pays taxes on 2% of its earnings.[75] The numbers for its competitor, Chevron, are similar: 75% of the oil and 80% of the pipeline business are in America, but only 13% of the earnings are declared in the U.S. The extraction of local resources and the environmental burden is not reflected in the low tax paid.

This is a trend you can see in a variety of industries. Bank of America generates 84% of its business in the U.S. and only declares 31% of its profits to the IRS. Citicorp creates 43% of its business in the U.S. and declares only 3% of its earnings to the Federal Government. The list of companies that report conspicuously little-to-no taxable earnings in the U.S. includes many on the *Fortune 500* ranking. The new tax law will soon show whether a reconsideration or elimination of all the peculiar loopholes of the old legislation will lead to a more fairly balanced tax burden.

Competitive pressure is something that has long encouraged companies to take advantage of tax loopholes. In fact, this situation has often been brought about by a company's own lobbying efforts. Apple's CEO Timothy D. Cook, for example, speaking for all corporations during a 2013 hearing before the Senate Permanent Subcommittee on Investigations, said: "We pay all the taxes we owe."[76]

The corporate principle is to avoid taxes no matter what, while readily enjoying the nation's infrastructure, such as the roads, bridges, airports, and hospitals, which are all funded by taxes. The available level of education, as well as basic research and development, are also tax-funded. Corporations rely on the

---

[75] Paul Buchheit, "How American Corporations and the Super Rich Steal From the Rest of Us," *AlterNet,* December 28, 2014. Buchheit bases his statements on SEC information for 2014.

[76] Newsmax: "Apple CEO Tells Senate: 'We Pay All the Taxes We Owe,'" *Bloomberg News,* May 21, 2013.

country's legal security and protection of material and intellectual property without paying taxes for it. It was easy for Timothy D. Cook to prove that his company simply took advantage, and made use of, existing laws to reduce his company's tax burden.[77]

It is clear that attractive tax legislation and concise, simple regulations would make U.S. tax loopholes obsolete. Tax reduction for American companies would bring manufacturing, jobs, and other activities back into our country. However, big corporations and very wealthy individuals continue to dominate the political scene. Medium-sized companies, as well as the average American individual taxpayer, are all taxed to the fullest and can rarely count on tax relief and loopholes.[78] They do not have enough representation in Congress, as compared to large corporations or the super-rich.

To understand the controversy of legislation, remember that U.S. contracts are based on Anglo-Saxon contract law, which does not refer to articles or paragraphs of law. In every American contract, the basics and all binding particulars are mentioned comprehensively, which results in a thick document. In each case, the letter of the law or the contract is what counts, not the intent and purpose of a provision. These detailed and long contracts are an invitation to incorporate inclusions and exemptions in favor of special interests. These are the famous loopholes to legislation.

In European civil law, regulations and contracts are based on one or several fundamental books of law. Contracts have to mention only the valid paragraphs that are specified in the law

---

77   Kevin McCoy, "Apple CEO defends tax tactics at Senate Hearing," *USA TODAY*, May 26, 2013.
78   Elizabeth Warren, "The Tax Code Is Rigged," http://elizabethwarren.com/blog/corporateinversions, August 1, 2014.

book to be considered legal and binding. This efficient system goes back to the Romans and was reintroduced to Europe by Napoleon Bonaparte.

Donations or Taxes?

In America, donating to charitable causes is a widespread activity and is generally a commendable action. Individuals, couples, families, and foundations donate time and money to various causes and projects. Understandably, they often want recognition for their generosity. This may be in the form of dedications, as in the case of Colorado's Calaway Young Cancer Center in Glenwood Springs, New York's Solomon R. Guggenheim Museum, or the Walt Disney Concert Hall in Los Angeles. At universities such as Harvard, Cornell, Brown, and Yale, libraries, churches, and scholarships have all been named in honor of a charitable donor. In my neighborhood, almost every public bench is named after a local character.

It is undisputed that donations to the fine arts, the sciences, and communities are intended for the general good. It is normal—and an integral part of the American psyche—for wealthy Americans to share some of their riches with the less fortunate. Former Secretary of Labor (under the Clinton administration) Robert Reich has written that the act of making a public donation has more than positive impacts:

Not long ago I was asked to speak to a religious congregation about widening inequality. Shortly before I began, the head of the congregation asked that I not advocate raising taxes on the wealthy.

He said he didn't want to antagonize certain wealthy congregants on whose generosity the congregation depended.

I had a similar exchange last year with the president of a small college who had invited me to give a lecture that his board of trustees would be attending. "I'd appreciate it if you didn't criticize Wall Street," he said, explaining that several of the trustees were investment bankers.

It seems to be happening all over.

A non-profit group devoted to voting rights decides it won't launch a campaign against big money in politics for fear of alienating wealthy donors.

A Washington think-tank releases a study on inequality that fails to mention the role big corporations and Wall Street have played in weakening the nation's labor and antitrust laws, presumably because the think-tank doesn't want to antagonize its corporate and Wall Street donors.

A major university shapes research and courses around economic topics of interest to its biggest donors, notably avoiding any mention of the increasing power of large corporations and Wall Street on the economy.

It's bad enough that big money is buying off politicians. It's also buying off non-profits that used to be sources of investigation, information, and social change, from criticizing big money.

Other sources of funding are drying up. Research grants are waning. Funds for social services of churches and community groups are growing scarce. Legislatures are cutting back university funding. Appropriations for public television, the arts, museums, and libraries are being slashed.

So, what are non-profits to do?

"There's really no choice," a university dean told me. "We've got to go where the money is."

And more than at any time since the Gilded Age of the late nineteenth century, the money is now in the pockets of big corporations and the super wealthy.

So the presidents of universities, congregations, think-tanks, [and] other nonprofits are now kissing wealthy posteriors as never before.

But that money often comes with strings.

When Comcast, for example, finances a non-profit like the International Center for Law and Economics, the Center supports Comcast's proposed merger with Time Warner.

When the Charles Koch Foundation pledges $1.5 million to Florida State University's economics department, it stipulates that a Koch-appointed advisory committee will select professors and undertake annual evaluations.

The Koch brothers now fund 350 programs at over 250 colleges and universities across America. You can bet that funding doesn't underwrite research on inequality and environmental justice.

David Koch's $23 million in donations to public television earned him positions on the boards of two prominent public-broadcasting stations. It also guaranteed that a documentary critical of the Koch empire didn't air.

As Ruby Lerner, president and founding director of Creative Capital, a grant making institution for the arts, told the New Yorker's Jane Mayer, "self-censorship" practiced by public television ... raises issues about what public television means. They are in the middle of so much funding pressure.[79]

---

[79]   Robert Reich, "Colleges, Churches and Non-Profits Doing the Wealthy's Dirty Work," *AlterNet*, April 7, 2015.

Reich is pointing out how donations are influencing and undermining the values of non-profit organizations, churches, and universities. Donors of large sums define the specific field of study or research, possibly controlling a certain outcome. The statement of "we have to go where the money is" is leading research and education away from critical issues. In the case of the Koch brothers—acting as Koch Industries, a leader in the oil business—professors may not be hired or promoted if they discuss the negative effects of fracking on the environment.[80] Research on poverty or social services, as well as insight and discussion into other sensitive and pressing scientific issues, may all be ignored or neglected. This is a no-win situation and zero-sum game for the American people... whose art, education, entertainment, and government are being paid for, to a huge extent, by corporations. Their intention to avoid paying taxes and influencing political life by its donations is what gives Corporate America a leading role in undermining the spirit of democracy.

Welcome to Absurdistan: America Under Corporate Rule

Who is to blame for this lopsided equation? And who is supposed to fix it? Nobody wants to shoulder the weight. In the words of one of the executives of Apple: "We don't have an obligation to solve America's problems."[81] For corporations like Apple and

---

[80] Dave Levinthal, "Koch foundation proposal to college: Teach our curriculum, get millions," *The Center for Public Integrity*, September 12, 2014.

[81] Charles Duhigg and Keith Bradsher, "How the U.S. Lost Out on iPhone

General Electric, priorities entail producing excellent products, selling them, and making a profit. In a way, that's how it should be. Companies are not empires. Businesses are not meant to replace governments.

Cutting Costs by Any Means Necessary

In the late 1990s, a change in tax rules allowed multinationals to avoid taxes on several kinds of banking and insurance incomes, creating an avalanche of restructuring accounting practices for tax filing. This tax break, known as "active financing", was a boon for big thriving businesses, especially for "investment banks, brokerage firms, auto and farm equipment companies, and lenders like GE Capital. This tax break allowed GE [General Electric] to avoid taxes on lending income from abroad and permitted the company to amass tax credits, write-offs, and depreciation."[82] GE led the pack by financing the sale of an engine in Ireland and filing the interest income as taxable in a foreign country—and, indeed, no tax was due in the U.S. because the profit was declared offshore. What GE initiated years ago is now common practice in Corporate America.

Does this benefit the average taxpayer? Senator Bernie Sanders of Vermont observed in 2013 that one in four corporations pay no taxes. "The truth is that we have a rigged tax code that has essentially legalized tax dodging for large corporations," Sanders said. "Offshore tax haven abuse has become so absurd that one five-story office building in the Cayman Islands is now the 'home' to more than 18,000

Work," *The New York Times,* January 21, 2012.
[82] David Kocieniewsky, "G.E.'s Strategies Let It Avoid Taxes Altogether," *The New York Times,* March 24, 2011.

corporations."[83] On an international level, the U.S. tax system is competing with other countries' lower and simpler tax regimes. The Republican tax bill of December 2017 is said to be much lower for corporations and would therefore make these transactions abroad irrelevant.

And it is scandalous that large American companies like GE are using and benefiting from the American infrastructure, educational system, and government programs all while avoiding taxes to help pay for the same public services which they feed off of.

Congressional lobbying to influence tax laws in favor of corporate tax deals undermines and weakens the nation's livelihood and, consequently, destroys democratic values. Amazon's CEO Jeff Bezos, for example, is convinced that he owes nothing to his employees.[84] In the early 1990s, he looked for a location with low tax rates and found it in Seattle, where online sales require no sales tax. It was there that Amazon, with a minimum 6–8% advantage over local brick-and-mortar stores, set up shop.

Interestingly, while the city of Seattle offers a low corporate tax, it is also one of the communities that mandate a $15.00/hour minimum wage. That definitely takes the steam out the criticism that a higher minimum wage discourages business and increases taxes. But Amazon's sales outside the U.S. are billed via subsidiaries in Luxembourg, resulting in a minimum tax rate of 15%.[85] And sales on Amazon are making life much more difficult for American businesses that do not share a similar advantage. A Colorado bookseller recently told me that shoppers come into

---

[83] Jon Greenberg, "Sanders: One out of four Corporations pay no taxes", *PolitiFact,* September 26, 2013

[84] David Morris, "Hey Michelle and Barack..", *ante.*

[85] Morris, *ante.*

the store to look at books and then place orders on Amazon via their iPhones. This is an example of how the lower prices of online commerce undermine local small businesses.

Corporate America snakes through loopholes without considering how this affects the rest of the country. Corporate America takes it for granted that engineers are well-educated when they are hired by companies. Corporate America expects to use technical research that others have funded and slaved over but which the government provides freely for corporate use.

Thanks, Corporate America!

Corporate America believes that the nation's roads, bridges, and airports have been built to last forever. It transfers the manufacturing of goods abroad and, at the same time, seeks protection from the government for international business relations and intellectual property. The protection of the waterways for shipping goods safely around Africa is expected, demanded from, and provided by Uncle Sam. Every day, corporations benefit from roads, bridges, and international protection more than any other segment of the society—and yet they contribute less to it than any other segment.

How are these services and the infrastructure funded? Corporate America is not interested in this question; in fact, it couldn't care less that it moves goods around the country and the world at the expense of American taxpayers. Welcome to "Absurdistan"—or, if you prefer, Corporate Paradise—where all good things fall like manna from heaven and where free infrastructure and services are available without question. The quest for low taxation has turned into a national mania!

To make the situation even more insane, the manufacturing and distribution industries alone spend an average $1.6 billion lobbying the federal government for *even more breaks*.[86]

According to *Forbes Magazine,* there are 29 companies that pay millions for lobbyists but not a single penny in taxes.[87] The article cited a report by the non-partisan corporate watchdog group, Public Campaign, naming corporations that spend between anywhere between the range of $710,000 to $84.4 million on lobbying activity.

The corporations get a free ride because Corporate America likes to transfer property rights and income-reporting abroad, thereby transferring a big part of their tax burden to countries with low tax requirements. Who is paying for this paradise? Certainly not the corporations...

But surely you can guess by now who is.

American citizens have tolerated expenses and accrued losses that have been kicked towards the taxpayer wherever possible, while the resulting profits are seeping into large companies. The country is permeated with this doctrine, which truly is a breach of trust toward the American people. Citizens expect—as they very well *should* expect—corporations to pay their fair share in taxes for the use of preliminary and basic services.

The rules of capitalism are such that each individual is responsible for his or her own fate. Upon reaching the status of *entrepreneur,* the popular notion is that one seems to have "made it" or landed on the "right side of the tracks." In the case of many small and mid-sized businesses, however, this is an illusion because of the tax burden. Small business owners and sole

---

86 Opensecrets.org, Center for Responsive Politics. Lobbying, top industries, consulted on June 26, 2017,
https://www.opensecrets.org/lobby/top.php?indexType=i
87 Chris Barth, "29 Companies That Paid Millions For Lobbying (And Didn't Pay Taxes)", *Forbes Magazine,* December 14, 2011.

entrepreneurs certainly do not have the tax advantages that the super-wealthy and large corporations enjoy.

The irony in of all this is that small businesses are undeniably the backbone of the American economy. They account for creating more than three-fourths of the country's new jobs and are responsible for more than 44% of the country's private payroll.[88] Furthermore, for every dollar small businesses are spending for their activity, 68% goes right back into the community, compared with just 46% ensuing from corporate retailers. This is because small businesses are more likely to buy from local suppliers and other small distributors, thereby enrichening the economy of their local communities.

Where have we gone astray? Have we lost a sense of responsibility toward the greater good of the community? A government that overlooks loopholes that favor corporations will see corporations as a prioriy. U.S. Congress has wedged itself into the position of favoring corporate profit over the needs of the American people.

Income Distribution

U.S. productivity has increased steadily since the 1940s. Until 1975, weekly wages were similarly increasing and all wage-earning income brackets prospered. Since then, lower wage income, adjusted for purchasing power, has been stagnant. The split in weekly wage income is clearly visible starting in 1975

---

[88] Patrick Duggan, "Why Small Businesses are the Backbone of America," *Pacific Community Ventures*, July 15, 2015, www.pacificcommunityventures.org/2015/07/15/why-small-businesses-are-the-backbone-of-america/

(see chart below). Since then, the wage-earning income development has diverged.

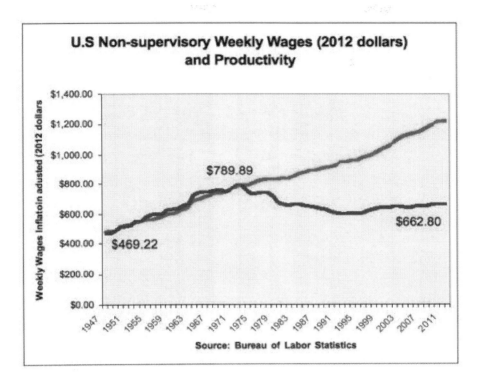

AlterNet:[89] **Weekly wages (blue), inflation-adjusted for 2012 in comparison to the rise in productivity (red).**

In the lowest fifth of the income bracket, payments rose from $17,663 in 1967 to $20,262 in 2011, which corresponds to an annual increase of 0.12% or 14% over the entire period. The maximum reached $23,404 in 2000. By comparison, income in the top fifth percentile climbed from $111,866 in 1967 to $186,000 in 2011—that is an increment of 1.12% annually or

---

[89] Les Leopold, "The 6 Economic Facts of Life in America That Allow the Rich to Run off with our Wealth," *AlterNet,* December 16, 2014.

66% overall.[90] From 1975 to 1980, the middle class began to dwindle. Low-income earners' income remained low as the rich became richer and transformed into the super-rich (or "the 1%" of the population).

> *The imbalance of wealth and power in our system is compounding. Those with great wealth are rigging the economic game through their lobbying, political contributions, and propaganda machines. (They're close to repealing the estate tax; close to getting the Trans-Pacific Partnership; Wall Street is rolling back the Dodd-Frank law; hedge-fund managers keep their "carried-interest" tax loophole; Big Oil continues fracking despite its environmental damage.)*
>
> *All this gives [the wealthy] even more wealth, which further empowers them to rig the game, leading to further wealth. (The Koch political machine alone has raised almost $1 billion for the upcoming election.)*
>
> *Average Americans, meanwhile, are falling further behind. (Wages are still going nowhere; pensions are disappearing; more workers are "independent contractors" with no Social Security, minimum wage, workers' compensation, 40-hour workweek, or unemployment benefits; college costs are skyrocketing, as is student debt; childcare costs are exploding; state sales taxes are rising even as income taxes on the rich are falling.)*
>
> *Why isn't this growing imbalance of wealth and power being talked about? Why isn't the media focusing on it? Why aren't presidential aspirants mentioning it?*
>
> *-Robert Reich, Facebook, April 5, 2015*

---

[90] Wikipedia, Keyword: "Household Income in the United States," consulted May 28, 2015.

The Middle Class is Disappearing

America is proud of its wealth and sees itself primarily as the land of the middle class. For decades after WWII, hard work allowed a large number of citizens to reach a standard of living that included a house, a car, and a "full fridge." The purchasing power of these people stimulated the economy. Since about 1990, however, job losses from outsourcing production and services to the Far East and Mexico have become noticeable and have changed the entire society.

In fact, the North American Free Trade Agreement (NAFTA) led to massive job relocations away from the United States. Contact with China, rekindled by President Richard Nixon, did not result in political rapprochement. Instead, it created economic competition abroad, with vast job transfers to the Far East. A new income class began to emerge at home: the working poor.

Economic data proves that the American middle class has diminished while the multitudes of the rich and the poor have increased. Conservative business associations claim that these facts are misrepresented and they are eager to prove that extreme income inequality does not exist. The American Enterprise Institute asserts, without quoting figures, that differences in income have narrowed since 1989; it furthermore dares to question whether the lower income segment is paying its share of taxes.[91] *The Federalist* declares that, "income inequality is good for the poor."[92] The Reason Foundation recommends teaching "tolerance for inequality."[93] Depending on

---

[91] Paul Buchheit, *ante.*
[92] Scott Winship, "Income Inequality is Good For The Poor," *The Federalist,* November 5, 2014. The article raises the rhetorical question of whether the U.S. wants to copy Europe's social legislation or remain a free country.

political attitude, these catchphrases are either important arguments or biting sarcasm.

So, what do we mean by "middle class"? There are many different theories for defining the middle class, and the numbers may vary widely. According to economic statistics, the middle class is between the first and fifth income quintile[94]—for 2013, that would mean middle class income is somewhere between $26,000 and $77,000.[95] Other definitions classify the middle class as having income available for insurance, healthcare, and retirement funds aside from the basic costs of living. Enjoying a "secure" income is another definition of "middle class."

In her 2014 article in *USA Today*, Erika Rawes listed the things the middle class can no longer afford. She reported that people have to choose between a vacation or major purchase, entertainment, restaurants, or clothes. A vehicle valued at $30,000 is well out of reach. Her definition of "today's bourgeoisie" includes "laborers and skilled workers, white collar and blue collar workers, many of whom face financial challenges" even though they're not living hand-to-mouth and season-to-season as the poor are.[96]

In 1980, average credit card debt was $1,540, or 7% of an average annual income of $21,000. In 2013, the amount owed to credit cards jumped to $9,800, or 13% of an average annual income of $72,600.[97] Consider, too, the amounts of student loan debt, auto loans, mortgages, and medical debts. For the average

---

[93] Buchheit, *ante.*
[94] Erika Rawes, "7 things the middle class can't afford anymore," *USA TODAY*, October 25, 2014.
[95] The U.S. Census Bureau. Average income for 2013 is $51,939, 8% less than in 2007. Published on http://en.wikipedia.org/wiki/Household_income_in_the_United_States.
[96] Erika Rawes, *ante.*
[97] Rawes, *Ibid.*

American household, debt has grown faster than disposable income.

Rawes added that savings accounts for unemployment, illness, accidents, and home damage hardly exist. Americans save very little for retirement apart from mandatory Social Security. 20% of the nation's 65-year-olds have no retirement funds whatsoever, and 59% believe they do not have enough savings to enjoy a relaxed retirement. Health insurance premiums and dentists' bills add to the unexpected expenses. Rawes pointed out that General Motors, the largest employer in the U.S. 50 years ago, used to pay an hourly wage of $50 (as adjusted to today's purchasing power). In contrast, Walmart—today's largest employer—pays about $10.

On the other hand, Paul Krugman notes that a large number of Americans think the poor are living on "Easy Street" because of all the government support they receive.[98] Two-thirds of all conservatives share that opinion; this attitude certainly influences politics. In states with Republican-controlled governments, the expansion of Medicaid programs is hampered even if the Federal Government pays the bill. Krugman says that punishment of poor people has become a goal.

The war on poverty has been a problem for decades. The goal of fighting poverty is to implement a nationwide level of welfare for a majority of residents. Many presidents—and the majority of them being Democratic—launched grand programs to reach that target, including Theodore Roosevelt's "New Nationalism", Woodrow Wilson's "New Freedom", Franklin D. Roosevelt's "New Deal", and Lyndon B. Johnson's "Great Society". Unfortunately, poverty has not gone away;[99] Medicare, Medicaid,

---

[98] Paul Krugman, "The Insecure American," *The New York Times*, May 29, 2015.

[99] Grover Norquist ("Americans for Tax Reform"), points out in a portrait of

the Older American Act, and educational programs from the Johnson Administration are still in use today.[100] It is a fact that, since Johnson's presidency (1963–1969), billions of dollars have been spent without really improving anything.

The Distribution of Corporate Profits Explained

Ever since Ronald Reagan's presidency (1981-1989), the growing income disparity has been evident. The compensations of CEOs and top executives have exploded, particularly since the 1990s, compared to the average salary. Manager compensation has developed a dynamic of its own over the last two decades.

Granted, compensation for top managers is an important aspect of securing a company's future. It is often difficult to justify the compensation paid in the form of bonuses. After all, "reasonable amounts" and "fair allocations" are judgment calls. If business capital belongs to a family, disposal and allocation are limited in most cases. Responsibilities change fundamentally when a company raises its capital needs by going public. Sooner or later, the responsibilities for the company's management are severed from the founder family and transferred to outsiders.

In the U.S. and throughout the world, it has become customary to allow top management to participate in a company's success in the form of stock options. It makes sense to

Thomas Piketty that the Federal Government has spent over $20 billion since the inception of President Johnson's "Great Society," with the objective of eradicating poverty. One out of six Americans, however, is still affected by poverty, and the relatively high base-rate continues. See "Thomas Piketty, Chronicler of Inequality," *Time Magazine*, April 27 and May 5, 2015, p. 149.

[100] Wikipedia, "The Great Society" [consulted April 23, 2015].

pay top management on the basis of success, as a way to foster effort and identification with the company. However, many top executives have used their positions to receive gigantic salaries and exit salaries. In the end, these salaries and bonuses cannot be justified by performance.

On the other hand, Economics professor William Lazonick points out that the success stories of some firms, such as Apple Inc. and the iPhone, are hardly due to the sheer innovative spirit of the company's own engineering skills.[101] Success is the result of a basket of knowledge, including inventions and ideas from various sources.[102] It is the result of publicly-funded, basic research projects that, in their totality, lead to prominent innovation.

Corporations no longer use the "Old Economy" model of tying their employees to the company with long-term contracts that include pay raises and pension plans. The modern information and communication technology companies have a corporate culture that embraces turnover, quickly replacing their older employees with younger people who command new technologies. People are hired and fired frequently. "Old Economy" companies have had to stand their ground against "New Economy" startups. A change in strategy has occurred.

Corporations now pay less attention to their products and employees and more to shareholders and stock market value. This is a fundamental re-orientation. In the name of shareholder value, new objectives have been set. The performance-based pay for top management is now tied to the stock market price. The

---

[101] William Lazonick, "Profits without Prosperity," *Havard Business Review,* September 2014.
[102] Lynn Parramore, "Lazonick: How Superstar Companies Like Apple Are Killing America's High Tech Future," *The Institute for New Economic Thinking,* December 9, 2014.

price of the stock has become the principal criterion for determining success.

Meanwhile, share buybacks and staff cutbacks—with severance packages for former top management—have increased the stock's price. Just like performance-based pay, the value of a company is no longer based on innovation and improved products. Instead, it is determined by the stock market value, corporate performance, and profits at the end of the quarter. Speculators, as well as managers, seek higher market prices for their stock. Lazonick shows the shift from a "retain and reinvest" process to a "downsize and distribute" mentality. Rewarding the know-how and experience of employees with good pay and pension funds has been replaced with short-term reductions of expenditures for fast profits. This has led to extremely high compensation for a few top managers, leaving the rest of the employees behind. It has resulted in further erosion of the middle class.

Reduced tax revenue for government, however, might lead to cuts in publicly-funded research. The biggest U.S. corporations listed on the New York Stock Exchange take advantage of publicly-funded research and development (R&D), which is free. One would expect them to pay for some of that cost through paying taxes. Their own R&D expenditures are tax deductible, however, which reduces their tax bills. In general, research is underfunded and underused, and the vast human capital is being neglected. This is a great threat to America's innovative strength.

What we are dealing with here are individuals who are out to fill their own pockets, presiding with a "what's in it for me" mentality. In his article "Profit Without Prosperity," Lazonick points to the momentum of market capitalization and distinguishes between buyers and sellers of large or small packages of shares.[103] He refers to those who are interested only in the difference between the buying and selling price of shares to increase their personal wealth as *traders*. On the other hand, *investors* are those who look at a company as a production or service-rendering facility, with management, employees, assets, intellectual properties, and market potential.[104] The differentiation between stock dealing and investment has great consequences and is essential for analyzing problems.

A well-known debate on the topic of market value took place in 2014 between financier Carl Icahn and Apple CEO Timothy D. Cook.[105] It appeared that Icahn was not happy with the value of his block of Apple shares. He asked the company boss to raise the price of its stock quickly and sharply by executing a stock buyback program. Two share buybacks were carried out, using part of Apple's European cash assets. Apple initially borrowed $60B, and later $30B, to finance the two re-purchases. This financial transaction is purely a manipulation of the share price via the stock market. To quote Lazonick: "Massive buybacks reward those who have contributed the least to Apple's products and profits. Icahn has contributed absolutely nothing to Apple's success."[106] Put bluntly, financial transactions *per se* do not lead to substantive profits in the sense that more or better products or services have been created and sold. Instead, they lead to profit-taking due solely to higher stock prices. Added value is only achieved by increased productivity and market success.

For a tycoon like Carl Icahn, who generates his income from speculation, the exchange value is the absolute value. Stock market trading wears two hats: one for the investors who are

---

[103]   William Lazonick, *ante*.

[104]   Parramore, *ante*.

[105]   Joe Nocera, "Carl Icahn's Bad Advice," *The New York Times,* October 24, 2014.

[106]   Nocera, *Ibid.*

willing to buy a share in a company, and another for the speculators who are interested in short-term transactions. Investors, employees, and ultimately consumers have a vested interest in the company to realize technological change and to convert that into product improvements. The speculator, however, demands his share in the company's success without having supported the company's activities.

Share buybacks of listed companies are proposed by top management and are submitted to the shareholders for approval. They are financed with profits that should be used for human resources and basic R&D, or otherwise reinvested in the company's activities of products and services.

Between 2004 and 2013, 75 companies out of the Fortune 500 list bought back shares valued at $1.1 trillion and made cash pay-outs of $500 billion.[107] All 75 companies followed the "downsize-and-distribute" model, facilitating the manipulation of the stock's market price. Lazonick believes that this short-term strategy leads to the destruction of competitive capacity. Share buybacks only work for speculators. Discretionary capital should be invested in human resources, product range, or product quality.

In 2012, the 500 highest paid corporate executives received an average compensation of $30.3 million, of which 83% was in stock options.[108] It's worth noting that board members are just as interested in driving stock prices up in order to improve their own compensations. Managers, therefore, have a vested interest in keeping stock prices high.

The companies concerned made it known that the buybacks assured their sustainability. Lazonick clearly states that top

---

[107] Parramore, *ante.*
[108] Parramore, *ante.*

managers who are paid in stocks have an interest in using company profits for stock buybacks because an increased stock price will add to their compensation. "The very people we rely on to make investments in the productive capabilities that will increase our shared prosperity are instead devoting most of their companies' profits to uses that will increase their own prosperity."[109]

As aforementioned, share buybacks do not contribute to the companies' innovation capabilities—even worse, however, they weaken the finances. They are justified as a one-time measure in exceptional cases. Shareholders need to be compensated for their risk of holding the stock in the form of dividends and not by exchange-driven increases in stock value.

The consequence of such buybacks is a sequence of stock market rigging in order to qualify for tax reductions. *Huffpost*'s cultural theorist and author Lynn Parramore asks: "Why give tax breaks to people who actively manipulate the stock market, helping to ensure that they remain comfortably ensconced among the 0.1 percent?"[110] She states that tax breaks to companies are simply used to shift the income to the very rich. The broken tax code is part of the income disparity and the loss of middle-class jobs.

Lazonick points out possible triggers that can cause damage. The Security and Exchange Commission's (SEC) regulations fail to sufficiently confront the conflict of interest. In the U.S., share buybacks are legal in the free market. It is very likely that this boosts stock prices. Top managers who have a stake in the company's share price can pick the time and circumstances for the buyback. This is to their advantage.

---

[109] Nocera, *ante.*
[110] Parramore, *ante.*

Members of a company's board of directors are another critical factor. Frequently, one company's board includes the CEOs of other companies. Their position gives them access to drive up the price of shares by speculation rather than investing in new products or facilities. In theory, boards are supposed to be concerned with the long-term survival of the company. Most boards fulfill that without question.

If a CEO is a member of other executive boards, the temptation is to encourage these companies to proceed with a buyback following his or her model. These power positions support self-interest and, therefore, undoubtedly sanctions buybacks while ignoring economic consequences.

With respect to those networks, Lazonick additionally observes that large companies keep hiring the same consultants that promote the CEO's above-average reward, based on the price of the stock. Other indicators of the well-being of a company are often not being considered. Finally, the story comes full circle. The CEO's employment contract is well designed to back up his compensation under all circumstances.

In principle, the actual task of the stock market is to provide sufficient investment funds for companies through equity holders. In reality, the speculators are given too much attention. Between 2004 and 2013, the annual volume buyback action was $316 billion, which is more than the capital raised on stock markets in the same period.[111]

Until 1991, the SEC rule was that stock allotments from buybacks could not be traded within the six months following purchase. In addition, profits from such transactions were highly taxed.[112] The vesting period was abolished in 1991, as was the

---

[111] Lazonick, *ante.*
[112] Lazonick, *ante.*

rule that a company's share transfer office had to report publicly on daily transfers during a buyback program. These changes now allow managers to pick the time for the transaction and trade of their allotted stock, which could be considered as "insider trading."

To reinstall a better concept of fairness, according to Lazonick, a reintroduction of the vesting period of one-to-five years would help address this problem. Profit-related salaries should be based on the company's medium-term results and prospects for growth, not on stock price alone.[113] This is not in the interest of shareholders' rights, and it undermines a free enterprise economy.

In 2014, Lazonick contacted Apple Inc.'s Timothy D. Cook and offered suggestions on how to use the cash flow to secure the company's future.[114] He pointed out in an open letter that the shareowners are not the only stakeholders involved in improving the company's value: employees are part of the equation. Lazonick said that even the taxpayers are directly and indirectly involved, and that they should receive compensation in the form of taxes paid.

He furthermore pointed out that the payment of taxes would help renew infrastructure and advance basic research. Employees need to be motivated, encouraged, and revitalized to maintain or increase productivity and innovation by receiving continued education opportunities, creative sabbaticals, and financial incentives. Maximizing the shareholder value is unilaterally preferred to the detriment of corporate cultures. Lazonick challenged Cook to reject the current trend and engage his company in investing in public projects and research. I could

---

[113] Lazonick, *ante.*
[114] William Lazonick, "What Apple should do With its Massive Piles of Money," *Harvard Business Review*, October 20, 2014.

not find an answer from Mr. Cook, and Apple Inc. is still piling its revenues abroad. The new corporate tax code of December 2017 ignites some hope that at least part of this money might be transferred back to the U.S.

Private Prisons

In a 2015 piece for the *Washington Post*, reporter Michael Cohen noted that private, for-profit prisons have been in operation since 1989.[115] There are currently 130 private prisons across the nation, collectively housing about 157,000 inmates and collecting $3.3B in revenue. This prison labor costs pennies on the dollar compared to the open marketplace. Prisoners are paid slave wages of thirty to ninety cents per hour because the U.S. minimum wage law does not apply to prison inmates. Some familiar entities—including the military and well-known companies such as IBM, Boeing, Motorola, and Dell (among many others)—use prison labor at the extremely low cost of about two dollars per hour.[116] The longer an inmate is imprisoned the more profit the prison makes from the individual's labor. Obviously, this equation could easily lead to extended sentences and over-crowded prisons.

In fact, as Cohen points out, some contracts have a minimum occupancy clause with the state, guaranteeing minimum 90% occupancy. Three prisons in Arizona have a purchase guarantee for 100% occupancy, easily enabling them to conduct a profitable business. Using prisoners for cheap labor to make a

---

[115] Michael Cohen, "How for-profit prisons have become the biggest lobby no one is talking about," *The Washington Post,* April 28, 2015; and Vicky Pelaez, "The Prison Industry in the United States: Big Business or a New Form of Slavery?" *Global Research*, March 31, 2014.

[116] Pelaez, *Ibid.*

corporate profit could become a tempting invitation to keep prisoners in prison longer or to put human lives behind bars for petty crimes. Guaranteed contracts with state governments to keep a private prison at full capacity are unethical—not to mention, such behavior sharply collides against the Libertarian credo of reducing the influence of the state.

Here is another paradox. The crime rate in the U.S. is declining, yet prison populations are increasing. The smallest, nonviolent offenses, such as the possession of four ounces (113 grams) of marijuana, can bring draconian sentences, like a two-year prison term in Texas. In New York, if you steal a car and two bicycles, you face 25 years of prison.[117]

Are we losing the point, though? The primary purpose and goal of prison should be the (typically temporary) detainment and eventual reintegration of offenders into society after molding them into more upstanding citizens; this is a sharp contradiction to the for-profit business model that these prisons have apparently adopted. The reintegration of citizens is too delicate and too important of a task to leave to a corporation whose primary interest is its bottom line. A for-profit penal institution is absurd and unacceptable. Human lives are at stake!

Cohen wrote that the 2014 annual report of the Corrections Corporation of America warned shareholders that shorter sentences with longer probation periods or more lenient penalties for drug possession and illegal immigrants would affect their business—and ensuing profits—negatively. The report actually stated that "any changes with respect to drugs and controlled substances or illegal immigration could affect the number of persons arrested, convicted, and sentenced, thereby potentially reducing demand for correctional facilities to house

---

[117] Pelaez, *Ibid.*

them." Or, in Cohen's words: "the nation is, in effect, commoditizing human bodies for an industry in militant pursuit of profit."[118]

It is worth noting that in the United States—cited as "the world champion in imprisonment"—seven times as many residents are imprisoned per 100,000 people than in Switzerland: 612 in America versus 85 in Switzerland. Reporter Beat Ammann notes that U.S. occupancy is around 5% of the world's population, but 20% of the world's prisoners are in American jails.[119] These odd conditions have led to calls to modify the legal system and allow for early release of inmates who have been sentenced for non-violent crimes and who actively redeem themselves by displaying good behavior. It is certainly a work in progress, and it will remain a struggle to enforce justice when individual agendas and profits are at stake.

President Reagan's "Supply-Side Economy" and Its Repercussions

Current economic policy and its related political goals are still being strongly affected by President Reagan's economic policies. The demands of a "supply-side economy" are:

- Less government spending
- Reduced income and capital gain taxes
- Minimized government interference
- Curbed inflation with the Federal Reserve System (FED)

---

[118] M. Cohen, *ante.*

[119] Beat Ammann, "Der Weltmeister im Inhaftieren geht über die Bücher" [The worldchampion in imprisoning is re-examining the situation], *Neue Zürcher Zeitung,* October 7, 2015.

In 1980, the U.S. economy was under the influence of stagflation, the combination of high unemployment and inflation. The high price of oil presented an additional problem. A solid economic policy would seek to attain full employment and price stability; it is no surprise, then, that the Reagan administration sought new ways to treat stagflation.

The logic at that time was to create an excess demand of goods by reducing the tax burden for citizens. Doing so would strengthen purchasing power and largely make up for reduced tax revenue. The decreased cost of less government activity would compensate for a reduction in tax revenue.

The new laws indeed reduced tax revenue, but government expenditures increased, including defense spending. The source of tax revenue shifted from high income and capital to mid-range income and new investment projects. Furthermore, in an attempt to reduce government influence, the Reagan administration tried to simplify the tax system by limiting deductions. In the years following, inflation and unemployment fell while employment and the gross national product went up.[120]

Free market conduct and little government regulation were the tenet during the Reagan years. It was the president's intention to revive the free enterprise and turn away from Keynesian economic policy, which originated during the Great Depression and the Crash of 1929.[121] Principles of the U.S. economic policy and conservative politicians are still guided by

---

[120] Wikipedia, "Reagonomics" [consulted May 20, 2015]. http://en.wikipedia.org/wiki/Reaganomics.

[121] Economic theory by John Meynard Keynes (1883-1946), which encourages an active role by the government in creating and maintaining full employment and price stability, is a very influential theory that found great practical applications from 1945 to 1975.

this conviction. Indeed, it is sometimes said that anyone who cannot identify with these objectives is un-American.

Between 1981 and 1989, Federal debt rose from 25% of the gross national product (GNP) to 39% of the GNP, or from $789 billion to $2.19 trillion. Within a very short time, the U.S. had metamorphosed from creditor to debtor in the capital markets.[122] President Reagan admitted that the high national debt was a great disappointment in his presidency.[123]

Supporters of supply-side economics, such as the Libertarian Cato Institute, point to the lack of implementation of proposed measures, such as more deregulation or even lower taxes, as the cause of Reagan's economic failure. Other critics, like Paul Krugman, proved that decisions made by President Carter (1977-1981) and the Federal Reserve concerning inflation and unemployment, rather than supply-side economics, laid the foundation to resolve the stagflation in 1980.[124] Even though Reagan raised taxes twice, tax rates and Federal revenue decreased while government spending increased, and debt was accrued.

The results of Reagan's efforts were in direct opposition to the goals he declared earlier, and that created new problem areas which continue to exist to this very day. Even though the outcome of the supply side of the economy had apparently twisted results (lower inflation but more government, big Federal deficit, lower investments, a rigged tax code, etc.), the

---

[122] Leslie Cuadra, "List of World's Largest Creditor and Debtor Nations," *Financial Sense,* August 31, 2011.
http://www.financialsense.com/contributors/leslie-cuadra/2011/08/31/list-of-worlds-largest-creditor-and-debtor-nations.
[123] Wikipedia, "Reaganomics" [consulted May 20, 2015].
[124] *Ibid.*

old objectives and arguments are still in use. The Reagan legacy will continue to be with us for a while.

More recently, Republicans, mainly those affiliated with the Tea Party, have taken up the subject of a balanced Federal budget. With the exception of the budget surplus years—from 1999 to 2001, under President Clinton, with a Republican majority in the Senate and the House—all budgets since 1970 have been in deficit.[125] The Bush/Cheney (2001-2009), Bush/Quayle (1989-1993) and Reagan/Bush (1981-1989) administrations, all of which promised lean government and a reduced deficit, left the biggest holes in national finances. One of the best-known and most controversial measures was tax relief for top income earners. The claim was that such a reduction in taxes would improve investments made by the upper class, resulting in more jobs. Grover Norquist (along with his lobby, "Americans for Tax Reforms") was a driving force behind these demands.[126] The U.S. tax burden for individuals and businesses has declined considerably since the 1980s.

At first glance, that familiar statement "I am fiscally conservative but socially liberal" does not appear contradictory. In view of today's tax structure, however, the two values— conservative and liberal (as in social democratic)—are contradictory. Conservative fiscal decisions still have a twofold negative social impact: income inequality and persistent poverty. Fiscal conservatism supports the four principles of conservative government leadership: low taxes, lean government, little regulation, and a free market. To date, these rules have failed to fix the country's social problems.

---

[125] Jim Dexter, "CNN Fact Check: The last president to balance the budget," *CNN*, February 3, 2010.
[126] Americans for Tax Reform, http://www.atr.org/.

The Private Sector Myth

Much of the American public likes to hear that positive economic results are generated by the private sector without government support. If you take a closer look, however, you'll quickly discover that this isn't the case. For example, an enormous amount of funds from tax revenues flows into universities for basic research and into the order books of private companies. Since the end of WWII and the beginning of the Cold War, private firms in northern California's Silicon Valley have relied on substantial Department of Defense support.[127] The invention of the computer as a method of communication became possible through taxpayer-supported research funds for Stanford University, the University of California at Berkeley, and the U.S. Department of Energy's Lawrence Livermore National Laboratory. Well-known corporations, such as Cisco, Oracle, and Google, received orders from these sources.[128]

Most Americans are not aware that the vast majority of university and private research money is the result of federal grants. Universities rely on grant funding—from institutes such as the National Institute of Health—that provides economic support to graduate students and funds research that generates innovations in fields such as medicine and technology. These institutes provide invaluable grant support for small business innovations.

Taxpayer-supported research funds are supplemented by contributions from private circles, such as family trusts and private donations, which is how this new sector was able to establish itself. The false assertion that the government did not

---

[127] Martin Lanz, "Mit Uncle Sam im Rücken," [With Uncle Sam in your back], *Neue Zürcher Zeitung,* July 24, 2015.
[128] Lanz, *Ibid.*

have any part in the success of the U.S. economy belies public social spending and private sector profits. The phenomenal success of the communications industry did not happen overnight. It took years of action and effort by many players to generate the current boom. Apart from Silicon Valley, other centers of basic research and technology have equally benefited from government support, among them Route 128 in Boston and the Research Triangle in North Carolina.[129]

Successful companies in these sectors received money from taxpayers. Now they are known as "tax avoiders", because they have transferred some business activities and intellectual properties to foreign countries. Avoiding taxes has a direct impact on research funding and indirectly impacts the very same company.

Capitalism in the World

In principle, democracy and capitalism are interrelated; this fusion has been a decades-old reality in the U.S., Canada, Western Europe, Australia, and New Zealand. The Chinese have demonstrated that it is possible for a centrally-planned government to coexist with a capitalistic economic structure. The Chinese model of capitalism is an ironic twist and seemingly completely at odds with their Marxist roots. However, they seem to balance the contradictions of communism and capitalism, working them side-by-side rather well.

By contrast, the market economy combined with western democracy is less attractive for countries and companies outside the Organization for Economic Co-operation and Development

---

[129] Lanz, *Ibid.*

(OECD). Characteristics of American democracy are becoming more and more peculiar, protecting the strong over the weak and undermining the very doctrine of democracy. Democracy in Europe is likewise falling prey to other agendas; the European Union suffers from immobility and ineffective social legislation— the summation of legal regulations of individual states. The power of the unions in Europe prevents evolutionary development of society and economy. Uncle Sam on the sickbed and a sclerotic Europe are common international cartoons.

Meanwhile, big business owners and corporations use their power to pass legislation to further their own interests, ushering the rise of a plutocracy (i.e. government by the wealthy). The rudimentary beliefs of Libertarianism have come under the influence of the popular Tea Party, ultra-conservatives who would like to see a smaller government and fewer regulations. This, in turn, would give free reign to unfettered capitalism.

In conclusion, the rich and the big Corporations don't contribute enough, despite enjoying, as a "free ride", many of the benefits that countries and governments offer. The resulting increase in debt ends up serving primarily the rich. The middle class is entering a downwards spiral and, together with the poor, becomes dissatisfied and disgruntled.

The Government Must Be a Partner

A democratic government's priority ought to be the wellbeing of its residents by setting laws in favor of justice and equality. That might include regulations for pension plans, health insurance, and further assistance or guidance. It is the government's role to lead by example: to set standards and encourage private or non-profit companies to do the same and help promote the greater good. Americans need to restore the concept of "government by the people, *for* the people." The government of a *republic* is the elected authority meant to mandate *the will of the people.*

We, the American people must demand of our government exceptional services, authentic representation, and commitment. The government is in service for the people. Governing a country is not a sport's event with a winning and a losing team but a process to make the entire population the winner.

I acknowledge, Medicare enjoys a very high satisfaction rate among seniors—and yes, this is a healthcare system run by the *government*! This confirms that it is possible to receive excellent products and services by one government agency.

The switch in American values from collective to individual responsibility is the reason for the fundamental changes within this country since the time of President Reagan. In my opinion, this needs to be reassessed and realigned. Americans should care and look out for their fellow Americans. The spirit of our nation has to reflect this principle, and underlying principle upon which this nation was birthed to begin with. To stand together is certainly a solution that will enable citizens to overcome today's divided and dysfunctional situation.

A Society Divided: Hardworking or Lazy

Friends recently sent me an e-mail stating that there are, in reality, two types of Americans: one is busy and the other is lazy; one works daily and contributes to society, the other does not. Some Americans fulfill their duties as good citizens, while others don't. The clear message was: "It's not about the haves and the have-nots; it's the dos and the don'ts."[130]

The e-mail suggested that the country consists of either diligent or lazy people, and, while it is a given that extremes can be found within a society, the question is what is the ratio between the two. A classification of "lazy people" could mistakenly include those who have been incapacitated by accident or military action. The unemployed may be included unfairly; they can furthermore be broken down into the temporarily unemployed and the long-term unemployed. The former group reflects transitions in natural workplace fluctuations or economic cyclical trends, such as the massive transfer of manufacturing jobs to East Asia. The latter group is typically the result of poor education, a lack of skills, mounting despair over not finding work, and other reasons.

> "The biggest divide in this country is not between Democrats and Republicans; it is between people who care and people who don't care."
>
> -Rachel Maddow, Anchor
> *AlterNet,* May 23, 2015

The statements referring to lazy Americans claim that it is the difference in character that divides the country and, as a result, drives it to ruin. The authors of such statements say that this seed of contention needs to be uprooted. This outlook doesn't seem to be reflected in our nation's politics ...

The Republicans truly believe that there is a level playing field. In a perfect world, that would be the case. It is not a perfect

---

[130]   Private e-mail received from friends on January 15, 2015.

world, however: all things are not equal and the playing field is anything *but* level for millions of people.

The model of lazy vs. hardworking does not take into account inequality due to different geographic areas or basic human traits like racism, classism, or an unequal public education system that clearly gives some students a huge advantage over others. The advantaged walk an easier path of a privileged life, while a big part of the population struggles just to make ends meet.

As of February 2015, the U.S. unemployment rate was 5.5% and affected about 8.6 million people; it has continued to plummet since then (4,1% in October 2017). Compared internationally, the figure is low. Unfortunately, the picture is distorted, due to the fact that those who have been out of work for more than two years are no longer receiving benefits and are not included in the statistics anywhere in the world. The true number of the unemployed, therefore, is actually much higher.

Part 4:
The Broken Democracy

Political Deadlock in Washington

The U.S. has been a divided country during all of its history, one way or another. It continues to distinguish between the diligent and the lazy, or the working class and welfare recipients. A rift was created by the two main political parties, Republican and Democratic, who are fighting each other with brutal, extreme, and excruciating methods just to maintain or expand their influence. At the time of this book's writing, respective party followers are close to being split evenly within the population.

Because the party platforms are widely divergent, we can certainly speak of a divided country when it comes to political ideas. A consequence of this is neither party having a premise for compromise as a means to solve imminent problems jointly and amicably. In the 1980s, the Republican Party started to emphasize a strict party loyalty (which I'll return to in a moment).

The split and the ensuing negation of compromise as a path for finding solutions is a new situation for the country. Since the nation's founding, Congress has been the center of tough and verbose debates, intrigues, and procedural subterfuge spiked with lies, contrived accusations, and even brawls, but until recently, there has always been room for compromise in the end.

Today, the Republican Party is considered conservative, often advocating Libertarian concepts. Although it has been steadily shifting more to the right, the Democratic Party is still labeled liberal by many and has some social democratic objectives. Both parties subscribe to the democratic principles of free speech, free press, the right to assembly, and religious freedom, as stipulated by the U.S. Constitution[131] and the Bill of Rights.[132] Other principles include the protection of private property and the freedom to pursue personal and economic development.

Have a look to the two big parties nowadays.

The Democratic Party has a broad base of followers who are left-of-center, and who favor social welfare and a new healthcare strategy. Following Hillary Clinton's stunning loss during the 2016 presidential election, the Democratic Party is disoriented. The establishment branch is fighting to retain influence over the party. It is challenged by the progressive wing of the party, which is driven by the ideas of Senator Bernie Sanders.

During the Clinton and Obama administrations, the Democrats defended the government's work and sought to improve social programs such as retirement funds and healthcare services. They have lacked the courage to commit towards a better welfare system. The Democratic Party has moved so far from their progressive roots that in retrospect;

---

[131] The United States Constitution was written in 1787 and ratified by Congress in 1788.

[132] The United States Bill of Rights, which enunciates 10 civil liberties that protect citizens from government overreach, was incorporated into the Constitution in 1789. It was written by Thomas Jefferson and signed by 56 members of Congress on August 2, 1776.

Richard Nixon was more liberal in his time than any elected Democrat today.[133]

Because the Democrats have few liberal goals to show for the past two Democratic presidents, Republicans moved even further to the right and continue to resent President Johnson's Great Society programs and aspirations for lower taxes, an overall tighter administration, deregulation of all industries, and a balanced public budget. The party has mobilized Christian religious conservatives and supports President Reagan's supply-side economics. More and more concerns of the Libertarian Party are accepted, and their principles are strongly argued.[134]

Both parties consisted of conservative as well as liberal members until about 1990. Based on the open-minded political attitude of elected representatives from both parties, compromises were possible and solutions were found for the country, solidifying the reputation of America's respected brand of democracy. Today, that situation has changed. Corporate money has so permeated both parties that neither of them is now truly representing the middle class.

Former Congressman and Speaker of the House Newt Gingrich has been and remains a key player in polarizing the two parties.[135] As Thomas E. Mann and Norman J. Ornstein, the authors of: *It's Even Worse Than It Looks: How the American Constitutional System Collided with the New Politics of Extremism*, state: "Gingrich deserves a dubious kind of credit for many of the elements that have produced the current state of politics."[136] In

---

[133] Scott Porch, "Richard Nixon would be 'drummed out' of GOP today as a liberal: 'He passed as much social welfare legislation as Lyndon Johnson'" *Salon*, April 4, 2016.

[134] See Chapter "Libertarian Politics," below.

[135] Gingrich was a member of the House of Representatives from 1979 to 1999, and Speaker of the House from 1995 to 1999.

[136] Thomas E. Mann and Norman J. Ornstein, *It's Even Worse Than it Looks*.

their chapter, "Seeds of Dysfunction", the authors list several reasons for the current gridlock in government.[137]

Gingrich's strategy of party polarization, starting in 1978, was to criticize the Senate and House harshly, to depict the Democratic majority as corrupt and inept, and to present himself and the Republican Party as the rescuer. Thus, Congress's reputation was damaged and the anti-government party claimed a fast victory. It was the Republicans' intention to close ranks and present a unified front. The willingness to compromise with Democrats in Congressional committees and on the floor fell sharply. Congress was basically at a standstill. In public, they took on the part of system critics and pointed out corruption.[138] The plan clearly was to turn dissenters into enemies.

It took many years for Gingrich to attain his intended objectives. Supportive groups, specially prepared TV appearances, excessive criticism of Democrats, exaggerated statements on the Senate and House floors, disputes with the Speaker of the House, and the exposure of minor infractions or critiques of Congressional pay all helped Gingrich beat the drum for his Republicans and portray the Democrats as scapegoats. Democrats were put on the defensive; they responded with criticism and a rejection of Republican motions.

Polarized Parties and Voters

Gingrich has always worked behind the scenes to undermine the Democrats' efforts. Because of his strategy and its repercussions,

---

How the American Constitutional System Collided with the New Politics of Extremism (New York: Basic Books, 2012), p. 42.
[137] Mann/Ornstein, *Ibid.,* p. 31.
[138] Mann/Ornstein, *Ibid.,* p. 33.

the parties and their representatives in Congress are in a permanent election campaign. The first candidates for the presidential election in November 2016 made themselves known in April 2015. Beginning with announcing their candidacies, every word and statement coming from the candidates was under scrutiny and checked for inconsistencies and changes in policy. The media, especially television, are very active in this process.

The current status is that the two leading parties in the country are more unified within their parties than ever before. What may look like internal progress from the party's point of view, however, is at the center of today's stagnation. The parties live separate lives as two power blocks that are stuck;[139] there is little overlapping between their positions that would allow for any common ground to be opened.

Instead, party leaders are eager to report, "We have the agenda!" which means "We drive policy." That should be true only if the President and both Houses of Congress were ruled by the same party and could decide on policies without much consideration for anybody else. Likewise, party affiliation among voters is stronger than ever. This feeds into the vision cycle of each side harboring an intense dislike for the opposing party.

Following the recent 2016 election, the two main parties are basically in chaos. Neither one is ready to solve problems and reunite the country. And both seem to be dealing with some unintended consequences.

On the one hand, you have got the Republicans who find themselves reluctantly stuck with a non-conventional and controversial leader whom they seem to have hoped the primary

---

[139] Mann/Ornstein, citing Ronald Brownstein, "The Four Quadrants of Congress," *National Journal,* January 30, 2011, *Ibid,* p. 45.

system would have weeded out. The new president has turned out to be a real nightmare for the nation, incompetent and inconsistent in many aspects of his political responsibility. As for the Democrats, they were stunned by the loss of an election that was supposed to be in the bag; they appear still not quite sure about where to place the blame. The party is so divided within the spectrum between left and right, that unless they resolve the rift between the supporters of Senator Sanders and the rest of the establishment, they won't be able to reemerge as a unified opposition force. They will instead continue to be too busy fighting amongst themselves.

This goes far beyond the traditional partisan divide; new voter blocks—such as religious conservatives, pro-lifers, and those unhappy with the Federal Government (like members of the Tea Party)—see themselves as Republicans, while those who are in favor of social programs or gay marriage consider themselves as Democrats. It used to be that although conservatives and liberals disagreed, they were able to remain civil to each other. They compromised in details and achieved some solutions. This is no longer the case. For many Americans, politics has become purely a personal and angry battle of ideologies.

The American red-and-blue political map influences election propaganda. Uncontested election districts do not need to be worked as hard by the locally dominant party. Unused funds from these areas can be used for campaigning in districts or states that are teetering between red versus blue. These are called "swing states," which are typically the ones that ultimately tip the scales in determining the majority in Congress.

But why is there so much frustration? Are voters angry because they no longer feel represented by either party? The one thing that is certain is that Americans increasingly distrust their politicians and feel that they can no longer count on them…

Candidate Selection and Election Influence

Democracy is actually very vital in the U.S.—I counted 19 different political parties in the 2016 presidential election. Yet the political scene is still dominated by the Republican and Democratic parties, given that the entire process favors a two-party-system. As a result, although voters may feel that they really *do* have an option, they really *don't* because of constant pressure to support only one of the two major parties.

If a third party does manage to garner a substantial percentage of votes in a presidential election, these voters are basically shamed by repeatedly being told that they threw the election at the cost of the major party ideologically closest to the newcomer. For example, Democrats claim that Ralph Nader's Green Party took votes away from the Democratic Party in the 2000 presidential election, which ultimately caused Al Gore to lose the election to Republican George W. Bush.[140]

The message is clear: if you wish to gain influence, you have to join one of the two big parties. The idea that voters must vote only for a member of a major party is so engrained in our culture that, in reality, the third-party candidate has virtually no chance of election. The two-party system is actually a product of the way America picks its candidates. Before a general election, the candidates have to prove themselves within party primaries or

---

[140] Wikipedia, *The United States presidential election 2000* [consulted June 22, 2015].
https://en.wikipedia.org/wiki/United_States_presidential_election,_2000.

caucuses. The primaries are now part of the election campaign, replete with active supporters, media advertising, interviews, and campaign speeches.

There are closed primaries, in which only party members can vote, and semi-closed primaries, in which other voters are admitted as well. A closed selection of candidates favors contenders with more extreme party positions. The real election campaign is a beehive of interviews and campaign speeches, with print and TV advertising carried on simultaneously in all corners of the country.

Locally registered party members rarely reflect the value of the entire election district. Their opinions are often linked to those of party ideologues, which may be more extreme. On Election Day, the voter may have the choice of up to a dozen candidates and parties, but, ultimately, there are only the two big parties from which to choose a candidate who stands a chance of winning. Different individuals promote themselves as candidates and take their chances by running for election.

I do not dare to say how democratic the primary voting system really is. It is odd to see when big names or party official favorites are posted. Well before the presidential primaries even began in 2016, for example, the race was already considered to be only a contest between Hillary Clinton and Jeb Bush.

In 2016, however, voters rebelled against the establishment and the result was unpredictable and a complete surprise. In this regard, the 2016 outcome really was true democracy in action. Donald Trump, the 2016 Republican presidential candidate, was an example of a GOP party member who is far from the party's ideal choice.

The Democrats avoided what seemed like a serious primary; from the beginning, Hillary Clinton was anointed the nominee well before Iowa. Bernie Sanders was to be only a token obstacle that could easily be overcome—something that turned out not to be the case. His progressive message resonated particularly with younger voters, and Sanders impressively drew crowds in the tens of thousands.

Many party stalwarts are not prepared to vote for the other party due to family tradition or other basic values; the candidate's profile actually only plays a small role. If voters are linked by tradition to one party, they will rarely check the parties' candidates' values. It is possible, however, that they may help select a candidate for their district who hardly reflects their own concerns. Over the last few years, the Republican Party frequently elected candidates with extreme positions, such as those favored by the Tea Party movement, who approve of Libertarian ideology.

The reality of the two-party system is that the majority rule ignores those who voted for the losing party or some splinter group. That is the consequence of the winner-takes-all strategy. A strong fighting mentality has developed over the last few years—fighting for your and against the other. Only the strongest are elected and their opinions on the issues will influence the legislation. Other opinions and values are not acknowledged.

The situation today is that voters are very angry with the status quo and the division of the major parties. They would prefer to see solutions. The American people, like any other nation's citizens, feel most comfortable when they are presented with real, viable options.

Is there any respective hope on the horizon? *Associated Press* writer Nicholas Riccardi observes that "the anti-partisan groups acknowledge they're fighting powerful trends but say the alternative is accepting that U.S. politics will just get worse," further noting that "independent candidates can create electoral surprises."[141] Various groups of dissatisfied voters intend to rally new support groups for independent U. S. candidates in different states. The aim is to present less extreme-minded candidates to build up an independent fraction of Congress members who are willing to search for common solutions in fields like health care, infrastructure, and immigration. The Serve America Movement and Unite America Party (formerly the Centrist Project) will hopefully show up in many places on the electoral map in the near future.[142]

Party Politics: Finger-Pointing Everyday

The roots of modern negative and aggressive campaigning really began with Newt Gingrich in 1978, the year that Newt Gingrich was elected to the House of Representatives. It was then that a group of Republican senators attacked incumbent Democratic candidates with negative statements.[143] Mann and Ornstein comment that, in comparison to today, the exchanged words were mild, but the style was still the same: attack the opponent, exaggerate a little, add something ambiguous, insult the other candidate, and use untrue accusations. The opponent is thereby forced on the defense and loses momentum. The term of discrediting your opponent became popularly known as "swift boating."[144] Both parties have been using this strategy ever since.

The whole idea of winning an election is no longer a matter of having better solutions to the nation's problems; it has instead

---

[141] Nicholas Riccardi, "Washington infighting breeds new independent United States candida-tes", *Aspen Daily News/Associated Press,* January 26, 2018.
[142] Nicholas Riccardi, *Ibid.*
[143] Mann/Ornstein, *Ibid,* p. 32.
[144] Swiftboating as described in *Wikipedia.*

become a contest about how well you can discredit your opponent.

For better or worse, the election of Trump was American democracy in action. Voters were not going to tolerate an election swayed toward a Clinton/Bush race and they voted for Trump in revolt. Americans helped Trump defy the experts and pundits and even the polls which showed him far behind Clinton. The lesson of Trump is that voters want real and solid solutions. Whether or not those solutions are practical or desirable, they want them nonetheless. Feeding off of this energy and desire was the real secret behind Trump's success.

Mann and Ornstein once observed: "The pathologies we've identified, old and new, provide incontrovertible evidence of people who have become more loyal to party than to country."[145] In other words, a party's ideology becomes more important than the country's welfare; their desired outcome has to favor the party regardless of whether or not it is positive for the country. The main concern of politicians is to be in control of power or to govern mainstream opinion. To assert that you are right, even though you may have distorted the facts, is everyday politics.

Is the 2016 election a sign that voters are increasingly rejecting the two-party system and are calling for a more diverse and vital democracy? Perhaps. But those who are party loyalists are more committed than ever and struggling hard in order to preserve them, signaling that the two-party structure won't be revamped so easily.

A party's politics are recognizable as a matrix behind any politician's statement. For example, Jeb Bush, a 2016 Republican presidential hopeful, blamed former U.S. Secretary of State Hillary Clinton, a Democratic rival, for the rise of the Islamic

---

[145] Mann/Ornstein, *Ibid*, p. 101.

State (ISIL) as the result of the U.S. Armed Forces' withdrawal from Iraq.[146] In fact, Jeb's brother, President George W. Bush, ordered the withdrawal from Iraq, and the Obama administration carried out the decision—Jeb neglected to mention these details. Instead, he emphasized the failings of the opposing party, which resulted in a one-sided point of view, further polarizing the two parties. He disregarded the decisions made by his own party and ignored Republican responsibilities, blaming only the current Democratic administration.

His demeanor is just one of countless examples. Sketchy statements, made out of context and with an emphasis on so-called mistakes committed by the other party, help to gain media attention and win votes. Loud criticism of the opponent and quiet reservation when it comes to one's own failures is common.

Disproportional arguments and promises are another type of politicking. For example, voters have long expected a proposal on how to resolve the 2011 budget deficit of $1.2 trillion. During his 2012 election campaign, Mitt Romney was asked where he would cut the budget. He replied that he would get rid of subsidies to the National Public Radio and the Public Broadcasting System first.[147] By doing this, a savings of $445 million would have been possible, reducing the budget by a mere .012%.[148] Was this irresponsible or simply laughable?

In his memoir, *Duty: Memoirs of a Secretary of War*, Robert Gates wrote that members of Congress immediately change their

---

[146] Werner Marti, "Jeb Bush geht in die Offensive" [Jeb Bush takes the offensive], *Neue Zürcher Zeitung*, August 12, 2015.

[147] National Public Radio (NPR) is a radio network not privately owned and publicly funded by local contributions from corporations, foundations and individuals.

[148] Elizabeth Flock, "5 Things the Government Spends More on Than PBS," *U.S. News and World Report*, October 4, 2012.

opinions when a television camera shows up.[149] Their social behavior turns from understanding and conciliatory to crude and uncivilized as they put their own interests before the needs of the country. Their activities appear focused on their own reelection, and the favorable response of a public opinion poll seems to be of utmost importance. That's what it's all about, however: self-preservation through reelection. This is so important to them that the average congressperson spends more time fundraising than he or she does actually working on legislation.[150]

That is the reality of American politics.

Commitment to the party line by party members and members of Congress has had repercussions on the composition of voters since the 1970s. Mann and Ornstein wrote that emphasis on party interests resulted in voters becoming more loyal to the party than to the country—something that ironically parallels the party members' behavior.[151] This is true of both major parties.

The thing is, politicians seem to lack an overview of nationwide problems. The political decision-making process has stalled while the problems get bigger and multiply, including increased national debt due to budget deficits, the immigration dilemma, income distribution, pension and healthcare plans, environmental issues, and failing infrastructure ... just to name a few.

Part of the problem is that extreme positions, especially those taken by Tea Party conservatives, are overrepresented in

---

[149] Robert M. Gates, *Duty: Memoirs of a Secretary of War* (New York: Borzoi Book/Alfred Knopf Publishing, 2014), p. 387.
[150] Stacey Selleck, "Congress Spends More Time Dialing for Dollars Than on Legislative Work", *US Term Limits*, April 2016.
[151] Mann/Ornstein, *ante*, p. 101.

Congress, while the reasonable center or liberal positions no longer show up in the distribution curve. Today's situation is dysfunctional. I share the opinion of Mann and Ornstein.[152]

Sometimes, I receive e-mails from supporters of the Republican Party in which they tell me that former President Obama is the only culprit for the country's woes.[153] The senders often fail to see that a president's role is plainly limited; he has executive power but, in other tasks, he can only execute what the two Congressional chambers approve. In other words, the President, heading the Executive Branch of the Federal Government, has the right to make proposals and veto legislation, but the Legislative Branch is ultimately the authority that *makes* the decisions. According to Ornstein, the Republican strategy over the past eight years has been fundamentally to oppose President Obama.[154] Anything coming out of the Democratic corner has been demonized. Negative results are blamed on the Democrats; Republican accomplishments are praised, but not objectively assessed or checked for public benefits. In short, it is a blatant evasion strategy. Attack is the best defense. "In other words," write Mann and Ornstein, "anything that Barack Obama is for, Republicans reflexively oppose."[155]

Congress, in my opinion, is responsible for current problems—including the Federal debt, budget deficits, and immigration—and has postponed solutions for years.

---

[152] Mann/Ornstein, *ante,* Chapter 5, "Fixing the Party System," pp. 131 ff.
[153] These are mass mailings organized by a support group and sent via email.
[154] Norm Ornstein, "If Obama is for it, we're against it, even if it's good for the country," as quoted by Tamara Lytle, in "What is wrong with Washington," *AARP Bulletin,* December 2011, p. 16.
[155] Mann/Ornstein, *ante*, p. 18.

Economic Context

With every action, politicians determine the lives of their nation's citizens and are supposed to provide practical solutions to problem areas. It is bizarre to see the self-praise of Republicans, as cited in a Facebook post by Robert Reich that reads:

> "Employers added 252,000 jobs in December, making 2014 the best year for job growth since 1999. The Senate's new majority leader, Mitch McConnell, said yesterday [that] the economic uptick seems to 'coincide with the biggest political change of the Obama administration's long tenure in Washington: the expectation of a new Republican Congress.'
>
> McConnell's suggestion that the Republicans' November victory caused the economy to do better is like a rooster assuming its crowing caused the sun to rise. Had the Republicans not blocked extended unemployment benefits, an increase in the minimum wage, and infrastructure investments, the economy would be far better today than it is. Even the median household income would have started to rise."[156]

This statement reflects the inability of the GOP to connect the dots of economic theory and its effects. The economic facts are easily converted to use as slogans for party ideology.[157] Carnival barkers are at work.

It is more likely that the positive results in the labor market have been caused by measures taken some time ago. The

---

[156] Robert Reich, Posting in *Facebook*, January 9, 2015.
[157] Philip Bump, "Mitch McConnell says improved economy is result of 'the expectation of a new Republican Congress.' Um, probably not," *The Washington Post*, January 7, 2015.

Republicans' job market assertion reflects an exaggerated opinion of themselves and the divided political climate in Washington. The GOP ideology uses its rights to communicate its beliefs to the public, which, factual or not, attracts more voters and sympathizers. The Republicans take credit for positive economic results; negative results are shoved to the "other side of the aisle."

I do not agree with McConnell's statement. While politics and economy are interrelated, they function simultaneously in two different cycles. They act independently but rely on each other. Politics is designed to create specific laws to fulfill political goals. The intention is to provide citizens with a decent life. Both political and economic decisions have a long-term impact and seldom produce instant results that are sustainable.

Economic results are influenced by cyclical trends. Politics and economy follow their separate ways and act asynchronously. The good economic results of November 2014 are a result of the Obama administration—and the President deserves the praise. Instead, the Republican majority leader in the Senate takes credit for the Obama administration's accomplishments.

Gerrymandering: Redrawing Election Districts

It is a peculiarity of the United States that only Arizona, California, and Iowa have independent election commissions whose impartial authority guarantees a fair election process. In all other states, the state legislator—together with the governor—has the right to define Congressional districts as mentioned in the Constitution in Section 4. Each state has its own regulations. Sometimes different commissions have the right to propose.

In an ideal scenario, these districts would be drawn in a fair and honest manner and without political bias. That has not been the case. As the state government is formed by one of the major parties, the ruling party draws these lines; obviously, since the party does this itself, there is automatically going to be a conflict of interest.

At this point, danger lurks in the form of gerrymandering,[158] a redrawing of a voting district lines in order to give unfair advantage to one political party. As a result, districts are drawn in an often-absurd manner so that no matter who is running, Democrats will always win in certain districts and Republicans in others. The districts can be manipulated in order to change which party will most often be favored. For example, a heavily Democratic district can be divided so that portions of the district now include a heavy majority of Republican voters. As a result, the Democrat grip on a district would be shattered and would probably favor the Republican Party instead.

Below is an illustration of real changes to election districts and their effects on Congressional seat allocations:

---

[158] Based on the name of Governor Elbridge Gerry of Massachusetts and the form of a salamander, from the supposed similarity between a salamander and the shape of a new voting district on a map drawn when he was in office (1812), the creation of which was felt to favor his party: the map (with claws, wings, and fangs added), was published in the Boston *Weekly Messenger*, with the title *The Gerry-Mander.*

Gerrymandering, explained

Three different ways to divide 50 people into five districts

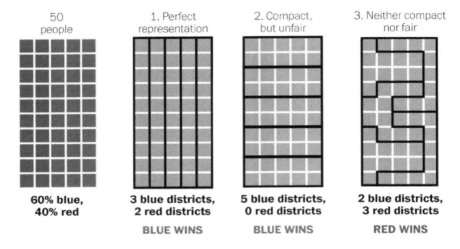

50 people	1. Perfect representation	2. Compact, but unfair	3. Neither compact nor fair
60% blue, 40% red	**3 blue districts, 2 red districts**	**5 blue districts, 0 red districts**	**2 blue districts, 3 red districts**
	BLUE WINS	**BLUE WINS**	**RED WINS**

WASHINGTONPOST.COM/**WONKBLOG**   Adapted from Stephen Nass

Stephen Nass and C. Ingraham, 2015.[159]

Gerrymandering is used by the majority party of a state to give itself an edge in allocating Congressional seats. It is a major contributor to current political polarization and the widespread sense that "the political system is unfair". If there are two equally strong parties, inevitably the majorities will change. When all is said and done, changing election district borders can lead to grotesque results.

Spent most of yesterday in Greensboro, North Carolina. [...] Greensboro is the state's third largest city, and still a Democratic

---

[159] Christopher Ingraham, "This is the best explanation of gerrymandering you will ever see. How to steal an election: a visual guide," *The Washington Post,* March 1, 2015.

> *stronghold (Democrats outnumber Republicans 2 to 1). But democracy is in the crosshairs in North Carolina. And with Republicans now in control of the state General Assembly, the citizens of Greensboro fear they're about to lose even their local government. A bill in the state legislature would change the City Council, replacing five Council districts and three at-large seats with seven newly drawn districts that would give Republicans a majority. It's the same story all over the state: Democrats outnumber Republicans, but because of gerrymandering [they] now hold only 3 of 13 congressional seats. The legislature is also actively suppressing the votes of minorities, curtailing early voting and imposing strict voter ID rules.*
>
> *Many of the same anti-democratic tactics are being used by Republican legislatures in Michigan, Wisconsin, and elsewhere around the country. For years now, the Koch political machine has quietly installed Republicans at the state level who are intent on entreating their power. They are actively engaged in what can only be described as a coup.*
>
> -Robert Reich[160]

Robert Reich stated that gerrymandering by the state of North Carolina, in this case, would determine the outcome of the next Congressional election—as it very likely did. In his example, the majority in the State General Assembly is one party, whereas the main body of voters in a local district tends to lean toward the other party. The electoral district is redrawn in such a way that the state's governing party gains a majority in areas where the opposing party used to be stronger. The outcome of future Congressional elections becomes, thus, a foregone conclusion.

---

[160] Facebook entry on April 8, 2015

I would hardly call that *democracy in action*. In the end, because of gerrymandering, we end up with a mish-mash of congressional lines drawn in insane, complicated configurations that favor one party or the other. This kind of partisan favoritism in redistricting doesn't adequately represent the true ideology of the people living in these districts. The most gerrymandered districts in different states show very special geographical forms, with some of the ridiculous allocations of regions ensuing in fascinating titles such as: The Praying Mantis (a Maryland district), Goofy Kicking Donald Duck (in Pennsylvania), or The Upside-down Elephant (a district in Texas). This only further exemplifies what a mockery of democracy this has all become.[161]

It should make sense that every state would use an impartial, independent commission to draw these lines. This is, in fact, unrealistic; in order to overcome the impasse, a state needs to pass legislation requiring it. Yet those passing said legislation would be the very same politicians who benefit from gerrymandering in the first place. Selfish as they are, why would they revoke that advantage?

American politicians do not reflect modesty and restraint; whoever has the opportunity to grab an advantage will do so. Gerrymandering, without scruples, turns a minority of votes into a majority of seats. In the 2012 presidential election, Democrats had the majority of the vote, but in terms of Congressional seats, they were reduced to a minority as if by an invisible hand.[162]

---

[161] Christopher Ingraham, "America's most gerrymandered districts", *The Washington Post,* May 15, 2014.

[162] Ian Millheiser, "The Supreme Court's about To Hear a Case That Could Make Partisan Gerrymandering Even Worse," *Think Progress,* February 27, 2015. Chart: David Wassermann, Cook Political Report

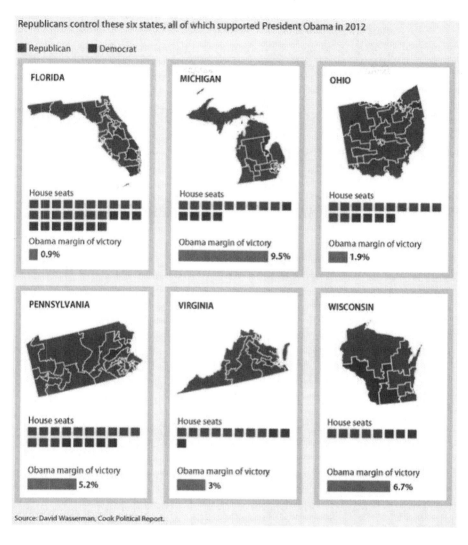

Republicans control these six states, all of which supported President Obama in 2012

■ Republican   ■ Democrat

Source: David Wasserman, Cook Political Report.

The above example shows how gerrymandering can easily turn a majority of Democratic voters into a majority of Representatives with Republican values. Gerrymandering thus becomes a legal way to rig votes.[163] The way it is handled in the U.S. is, in fact, a legal form of voter fraud.

---

[163]   Millheiser, *Ibid.*

Election districts should only be adjusted over decades and after the national census reveals clear migratory gains or losses. The implementation of an independent election commission for every state could solve this problem. Such an independent commission would have to be approved by the state's legislature, which would have to relinquish some of its authority. That, says Norm Ornstein, is not very likely to happen.[164]

As noted, only Arizona, California and Iowa have such election commissions, and a lawsuit is pending before the U.S. Supreme Court regarding the legality of the one in Arizona. According to the U.S. Constitution, "The Times, Places and Manner of holding Elections for Senators and Representatives, shall be prescribed in each State by the Legislature thereof."[165] According to Ornstein, should the Supreme Court stick to the letter of the U.S. Constitution, it would be almost impossible to get rid of the politically dubious gerrymandering.[166] Ornstein maintains that independent election commissions will create less polarization within U.S. democracy and reduce the cynicism within the currently unbalanced electorate.

Nevertheless, the situation is beginning to change. People for the American Way, a civil-rights watchdog group, found that Florida's highest court has annulled the existing election districts in order to protect against discrimination of black voters.[167] Reporter Michael Li wrote that a public vote to ban gerrymandering in Florida was held in 2010 and passed with a

---

[164] Norm Ornstein, "The Pernicious Effects of Gerrymandering," *National Journal Daily*, December 4, 2014.
[165] Constitution of the United States, Article I, Section 4.
[166] Ornstein, *ante*.
[167] People For the American Way, "People For The American Way Foundation Applauds FL Supreme Court for Striking Down Gerrymandered Districts," July 9, 2015.

62% approval margin.[168] This news is a ray of hope in this strangely deadlocked state of affairs.

Demographic Shifts

For several different reasons, America is experiencing a demographic shift that is changing the dynamics of the political landscape. Immigration and strong internal migration further polarize U.S. politics. Retirees moving to the South have reinforced Republican voters from Virginia to Texas. The defeat of incumbent Democratic Senator Mary Landrieu in Louisiana in 2014 suggests that this area, once dominated by conservative Democrats, is now firmly in Republican hands.

On the other hand, the pattern of people moving away from eastern seaboard states has allowed Democrats to dominate in the Northeast. On the West Coast, for instance, California, Oregon, and Washington have become Democratic strongholds. Immigrants from Asia, Mexico, and South America, who now live in these states, predominantly support the Democratic Party. A national blue and red map of party strength shows blue Democratic voters on both coasts and red Republican voters in the Midwest and the South.

In America, changing jobs across the country is very common and often requires finding a new home. You have heard the old saying: "Birds of a feather flock together." So it is with Americans when they're looking for a new place to live; they want a good location and quality of life, ideally in a neighborhood of like-

---

[168] Michael Li, "Citizen-Led State Gerrymandering Reforms Starts to Show Results." *billmoyers.com,* July 13, 2015.
http://billmoyers.com/2015/07/13/citizen-led-state-gerrymandering-reforms-start-to-show-results/.

minded people.[169] This is exactly how liberal or conservative leaning districts are formed in the first place. Democrat voters are more likely to want to live near other Democrats and the same is true of the Republican voters. Choice of residence could be said to reinforce the existing distribution on the map of party colors.

The Legislature's Modus Operandi

The division along party lines is par for the course in American politics and seems to have become the new norm of Congress' way of work. Mann and Ornstein make further suggestions about how to end the deadlock in Congress. They assert that many of today's Senate regulations favor the minority party, but many of the duties ensuring good parliamentary practice are left to the majority. In their opinion, the majority is entitled to the advantages. After all, voting favors the majority.

In cooperation with the President, the majority party should address the voters' major concerns. The minority will use various tactics to force its priorities, such as filibusters, calls for a quorum, motions to adjourn, and time limitations. A filibuster is one of the best-known dilatory methods for the minority. It is used to prevent a bill from coming to a vote by holding the floor during a Congressional decision. If a measure cannot be passed, time limitations stipulate when it can be brought to debate again. Reopening of a debate can be further delayed by a filibuster in order to break another time limit. If later amendments or substitutions of bills are discussed, they are subject to the same

---

[169] "Pew study finds more polarized Americans increasingly resistant to political compromise," *Rocky Mountain PBS, The Newshour,* June 12, 2014. [Gwen Ifill discusses with Michael Dimock.]

obstructive tactics. Thirty hours of discussion on the floor can be drawn out for weeks.

The use of the filibuster has increased conspicuously during President Barack Obama's tenure. Only 60 to 80 filibusters were used per legislative session during the Clinton and Bush administrations. During Obama's presidency, the number of filibusters jumped to 140.[170] In particular, confirmation votes for heads of federal agencies produced 38 filibusters under George W. Bush, compared to 81 under Obama.[171] Gridlock and obstructionism through use of the filibuster blocked or challenged the process almost every step of the way.

Mann and Ornstein believe these repetitions need to be inhibited.[172] A majority of the Senate can end a filibuster. In other words, if 60 Senators agree, a filibuster can be brought to closure. Mann and Ornstein suggest reducing that number to 40.[173] They proposed that confirmations of high government employees must follow standard procedures regarding time and hearings.

America's Political Protagonists

Congress is made up of 100 senators and 435 representatives. It is mandatory for members to disclose their finances. Records from the 114th Congress, from January 2015 to December 2016, show that the average wealth of Congressional members is above that of the average citizen.

---

[170] Kevin Drum and Jaeah Lee, "3 Charts Why Democrats Went Nuclear on the Filibuster," *Mother Jones,* November 22, 2013.
[171] Drum/Lee, *Ibid.*
[172] Mann/Ornstein, *ante,* p. 169.
[173] Mann/Ornstein, *ante.*

About half (268) are millionaires. While there is nothing wrong with successful and wealthy Americans making laws, it is ironic that, as Russ Choma of *OpenSecrets.org* wrote, "[the rich] are debating issues like unemployment benefits, food stamps, and the minimum wage, which affect people with far fewer resources, as well as considering an overhaul of the tax code."[174] Has the world's greatest democracy evolved into a cold, shameless political system designed to exploit the less fortunate? It is tempting to bend the rules to benefit one-self.

The Role of the Supreme Court

Appointments to the Supreme Court are made upon Presidential recommendation and are confirmed by the Senate. These appointments are for life, and Supreme Court Justices' terms are unlimited. Judges are often well-advanced in age and only leave the bench after resignation or death. Their influence is incredibly significant to the fate of the nation; they have the power to shape the lives of Americans for decades to come. Given their unlimited terms, the longest-serving justices on the bench may have been approved by a Senate some 30 years before, such as the late Antonin Scalia (appointed 1986) or Anthony Kennedy (1988). The principles and values of each judge continue to be reflected in judgments made decades after their individual appointment.

In theory, the nine Supreme Court justices are not affiliated with one of the two major parties, but it is not surprising that nominations are made along party lines. As a result, we have a

---

[174] Russ Choma, "Millionaires' Club: For First Time, Most Lawmakers are Worth $1 Million-Plus," *OpenSecrets.org*, http://www.opensecrets.org/news/2014/01/millionaires-club-for-first-time-most-lawmakers-are-worth-1-million-plus/ January 9, 2014.

Court that runs along partisan and ideological lines and is divided along liberal and conservative wings of the Court. The balance of the Court matters because recent history of the Supreme Court shows many close decisions, usually 5-4, which concern healthcare, same-sex marriage, campaign spending, and voting rights.[175]

The legal reasoning behind the 2010 Citizens United decision to lift political contribution limits has been a topic of many commentaries and speculations. Reporter Richard Hasen wrote that Justice Anthony Kennedy, for example, maintains that donations from companies do not give reason to speak of corruption or even a semblance of corruption.[176] Hasen added: "That statement, belied by the everyday experience of politicians and lobbyists throughout Washington, has opened the floodgates to even more money in politics, and more corruption."[177] The consequences of these large amounts of money that are flooding U.S. politics are frightening. Money can buy nearly anything— certainly including influence and power. CNN News anchor Erin Burnett called the 2010 decision a "Democratic and Republican bipartisan loophole action."[178]

As we consider American democracy, the role that the Supreme Court plays as a catalyst in forming and maintaining this semblance of democracy cannot be ignored. It was the Court judges and not Congress that changed the face of American politics with their decisions. The Court has the power to preserve or undermine American democracy; it did the latter

---

[175] infoplease: Milestone cases in Supreme Court History, February 27, 2016. http://www.infoplease.com/ipa/A0101289.html.

[176] Richard L. Hasen, "How Justice Kennedy paved the way for 'Super-PACS' and the return of soft money," *Slate*, October 25, 2011, quoted in Mann/Ornstein, *ante*, p. 73.

[177] Mann/Ornstein, *ante*, p. 73.

[178] CNN News, January 27, 2012, quoted in Mann/Ornstein, *ante*, p. 75.

with its decision regarding Citizens United v. FEC. This move greatly loosened regulations governing campaign finance law.[179]

Now, more than ever, the super-rich and big corporations are pressing for legislation that will keep the current regulations in place. Support groups like the many political action committees (PAC's) are common; by now, all political groups—be they Republican or Democrat, large conglomerates, labor unions, or political exponents—are using PAC's. This development began in the 1990s and has become an integral part of America's political environment.

Nevertheless, political scientists Mann and Ornstein are concerned about this process. They argue that this combination of old behavior, new technologies, new protagonists, and the effect of a new political culture has passed a critical point and will lead to something more worrisome than anything they have encountered in their 40-year careers.[180]

Politics and Wealth

Voting Rights and Elections

The U.S. electoral system is a representative democracy; every two years, voters elect their Representatives. However, voter turnout faces several obstacles. One obstacle is voter registration. In contrast to other democracies, which provide their citizens the right to vote automatically, American citizens

---

[179] "Citizens United v. Federal Election Commission," *Ballotpedia,*
https://ballotpedia.org/Citizens_United_v._Federal_Election_Commission
[180] Mann/Ornstein, *ante,* p. 80.

must register to vote. In other words, each individual must actively seek out the right to vote.

American citizens can only register to vote in person, at specific places and at specified times, with a few exceptions. On-line registration, for example, is offered in only ten states, even though it has plenty of advantages including better and easier accessibility, lower costs, and ultimately a greater voter turnout.

In Colorado where I live, citizens can register to vote at the polling place on Election Day. The State of Oregon changed the principle of passive voter registration with a law requiring state authorities to register all citizens based on their driver's license data.[181] In Larimer County, Colorado, simple voter registration in front of supermarkets and at other easily-accessible locations with adequate parking resulted in an increase of voters, which researchers Robert Stein (Rice University) and Greg Vonnahme (University of Missouri) call a boost for the average American citizen.[182]

Unfortunately, a proposal to launch a National Voter Registration Day has been rejected by mostly Republican circles, because they suspect it will benefit Democrats.[183] It is striking to see that many states with Republican governors refuse to consider different registration times and places, such as on Sundays in front of churches. Communities and states have practically denied citizens the right to vote, since these citizens do not have the time or transport means to show up at the timeslots and places decreed by the law, which civil rights activists have repeatedly decried as undemocratic.

[181] Robert Reich, Note on Facebook, March 18, 2015.
[182] Robert M. Stein and Greg Vonnahme, "Election Day Vote Centers und Voter Turnout," *Midwest Political Science Association*, Chicago, IL, April 22-24, 2006, in Mann/Ornstein, *ante,* p. 136.
[183] Mann/Ornstein, *ante,* p. 136.

The name of the game for any political party is to attract their own voters and encourage them to participate in the election process while discouraging the opposition's voters. However, when voter turnout is high, it tends to favor Democrats; when it is low, the outcome leans more towards Republicans. As a result, Democrats work hard to get their voters out through any means possible. Democrats fight for easy voter registration, early voting, and expanding absentee balloting. The Republicans, meanwhile, do their best to complicate the process of voting in order to restrain the percentage of Democratic votes.

Every citizen should have the right to vote. It is, however, surprising to see how restrictions against early voting, and the photo ID requirement, are practiced nationwide.[184] For some years, it was possible to deposit your ballot with the Board of Elections up to two months prior to the actual election, but the new photo ID requirement discourages many people from registering to vote altogether; as pointed out by NPR's Corey Dade, "many seniors and poor people don't drive. In big cities, many minorities rely on public transit. And many young adults, especially those in college, don't yet have licenses."[185] The PEW Research Center reported that close to 2.2 million Americans were denied the opportunity to vote in the 2008 election.[186]

Other restrictions are reflected in the following statements:[187]

---

[184] People for the American Way, "Report: In Key Races, Margin of Victory Came Close to 'Margin of Disenfranchisement,'" November 07, 2014.

[185] Dade, Corey, "Why New Photo ID Laws Mean Some Won't Vote", January 28, 2012, NPR, http://www.npr.org/2012/01/28/146006217/why-new-photo-id-laws-mean-some-wont-vote.

[186] The Pew Center on the States, "Upgrading Democracy: Improving America's Elections by Modernizing States' Voter Registration Systems," November 2010, in Mann/Ornstein, *ante*, p. 134.

[187] Jason Sattler, "6 Other Times Republicans Admitted Voting Restrictions Are Just About Disenfranchising Democrats," *The National Memo*, October 25, 2013.

- In Pennsylvania, the Republican Chairman of the State Assembly commented that the new voter identity card would allow Mitt Romney to take the state.[188]
- Florida's Chairman of the Republican Party said that early voting was restricted because it was not good for the party.[189]
- Former North Carolina Republican Don Yelton remarked on voting restrictions, including the requirement for a photo ID: "[We Republicans are] going to kick Democrats in the butt."[190]
- The Republican Attorney General of Texas and supporter of Greg Abbott's bid for state governor said, "Their redistricting decisions were designed to increase the Republican Party's electoral prospects at the expense of the Democrats."[191]
- Doug Preiss, the Chairman of the Republican Party in Franklin County (Ohio's second largest county), observed that Republicans would fight early voting decidedly: "I guess, I really, actually feel we shouldn't contort the voting process to accommodate the urban—read African-American—voter-turnout machine."[192]

---

[188] Pennsylvania Republican House Leader Mike Turzai said, "the new Voter ID, which is gonna allow Governor Romney to win the state of Pennsylvania, done." *Politico*, June 25, 2012. http://www.politico.com/news/stories/0612/77811.html.

[189] Dara Kam and John Lantigua, "Former Florida GOP leaders say voter suppression was reason they pushed new election law" (Jim Greer, "We've got to cut down on early voting because early voting is not good for us.") *Palm Beach Post*, November 25, 2012.

[190] Jason Sattler, *ante.*

[191] Ian Millhiser, "Texas Brags To Court That It Drew District Lines To 'Increase The Republican Party's Electoral Prospects,'" *Think Progress*, August 14, 2013.

[192] Jason Sattler, *ante.*

Are these the true reasons for the voting restrictions?

As aforementioned, even the actual scheduling of the voting process sets up many want to be voters for failure. Election Day, always the first Tuesday in November, is a curious remnant of the past. In 1845, voting dates were set according to market days and so as to not interfere with church attendance on Sunday. Today, however, some employees are often prevented, delayed, or even excluded from voting because of voting times and places.

The media use long waiting lines at the polls as proof of a living democracy. Mann and Ornstein report, however, that a quarter of non-voters give practical reasons for staying away from the polls, such as the timeslot when the poll is open or how inconveniently far they have to travel to vote.[193] Employed citizens with fixed working schedules and those who work far from their homes are at a disadvantage. So are those who, due to poverty or infirmity, find that even the shortest distance is insurmountable. In a true democracy, voting should be easy and assessable for all voters.

Why not shift the voting process from a 12-hour to a 24-hour period, perhaps even from Saturday noon to Sunday noon? Compulsory voting, more incentives for voting, or even penalties for not voting (a logical curiosity) could increase voter turnout. The basic notion behind setting a date for Election Day should be to provide as many citizens as possible with the opportunity to exercise their right. In all states excepting Arizona, California, and Iowa, the ruling party of the state government and local legislature defines the particulars of an election. Voter ID requirements, polling station opening times, and election district borders are set according to the wishes of the party in charge.

---

[193] Mann/Ornstein, *ante,* p. 140.

Election procedures in 47 states are subject to party wrangling and are not properly, democratically regulated. The parties are led by their objectives, and they are not concerned with correct and democratic processes. The interest of the party is more important than democracy or the needs of the American people. This sentiment seems echoed by some individual voters, too. In 2014, Tom Perkins, a successful businessman and cofounder of a venture capital firm, proposed limiting voting rights to taxpayers. He added that the rich, who pay more taxes, should have more voting rights than average citizens. A CNN report published his claims that "The Tom Perkins system is: You don't get to vote unless you pay a dollar of taxes."[194]

In 1965, in response to the Civil Rights Movement from 1954-1968, President Lyndon B. Johnson signed the Voting Rights Act into law to guarantee voting rights for all U.S. citizens and to eliminate voter discrimination due to race. The Act was designed to strengthen the 14th and 15th Amendments to the Constitution; it was an effort to insist upon citizens' rights, regardless of race, language, or creed. The law stipulates that state and community regulations cannot infringe upon Federal election principles. Changes on the Federal level require the approval of the U.S. Attorney General or the U.S. District Court for the District of Columbia.

Sadly, this hasn't been enough.

In *Give Us the Ballot: The Modern Struggle for Voting Rights in America*, author Ari Berman points out that in 49 states, nearly 400 voting restrictions were introduced between 2011 and 2015.[195] The restrictions were peddled as measures to curtail

---

194 Charles Riley, "Tom Perkins' big idea: the Rich should get more votes," *CNN money*, February 14, 2014.
195 Ari Berman, *Give Us the Ballot. The Modern Struggle for Voting Rights in America.* (New York: Farrar, Straus and Giroux, 2015).

voter fraud. *New York Times* reporter Brendan Nyhan explains that voter fraud, as such, is rare. The myth, however, is widespread.[196] Voter fraud in America is frequently debated in the media and courts, where actual cases of unauthorized voter registrations are generally proven case by case. The extent to which restrictions have been applied throughout the country, however, can only be explained by party interest and not by any real attempts to fight voter fraud.

Once again, party interest appears to be more important than fairness and equality for all.

Lobbying and Campaign Financing

Campaign financing has always been a controversial topic in America. Millions of dollars are spent on election propaganda during the primaries; afterward, an enormous amount of money is then raised for the November election. Contributions to municipal, county, or state campaigns are naturally more modest than those on the Congressional level. However, the questions of how much can be contributed, how transparent the financing should be, and who is allowed to receive contributions are all ubiquitous and ever-present, including the issue of whether or not recipients of government contracts are allowed to make campaign donations or not.

Since the founding of the United States of America, politics have been shaped by the influence of money on the law-making process. Many presidents made additional regulations to fight against this bias, and companies' contributions to candidates and parties were outlawed in the past. Exaggerated monetary

---

[196] Brendan Nyhan, "Voter Fraud is Rare, but Myth is Withspread," *The New York Times,* June 10, 2014.

contributions and violations of existing regulations led to stringent restrictions in 1972, limiting the financing of presidential campaigns. However, these bans have been gradually lifted.

In 1990, the parties found ways to work around these restrictions by collecting indirect contributions (so-called "soft money") that were not earmarked for presidential campaigns.[197] Dinners with a celebrity or a night in the White House's Lincoln bedroom were up for sale. The revenue poured into party accounts and not directly into election campaigns, blurring the boundaries between official and private interests.

> "A politician is a fellow who will lay down your life for his country."
>
> -Texas Guinan (1884-1933)

In 2002, Congress acted one more time to create new regulations by passing the Bipartisan Campaign Reform Act ("McCain-Feingold"). It forbids the collection of "soft money" and provides clear standards for advertising on the internet.[198] This McCain-Feingold Act barred corporations and unions from using their funds in order to finance issue advertisements which basically are propaganda ads.

In favor of the Citizens United Political Action Group (PAC) in 2010, the Supreme Court decided to lift all restrictions against donating wealth for political campaigns. This decision signaled a turnabout in party and campaign financing. Citizens United

---

[197] Mann/Ornstein, *ante*, p. 70.
[198] Mann/Ornstein, *ante*, p. 71.

essentially maintained that corporations have the same constitutional rights as people and therefore are permitted to donate unlimited funds to campaigns and candidates. This one move practically annihilated the McCain-Feingold Act and any prior serious campaign reform.

All efforts and restrictions for individuals, as well as business entities, in terms of direct or indirect contributions, were overturned. Nonetheless, the highest court's decision continues to be strongly disputed. Mann and Ornstein wrote that the decision in favor of the plaintiff, a donor group centered around the Koch brothers in the case Citizens United v. Federal Election Commission, "[has] created the political equivalent of a new Wild West."[199] Current regulations for support organizations and PAC's are vague and full of loopholes.

While the names of donors and contributors changed—from Carnegie and Morgan to the Koch Brothers or George Soros, for instance—the principal is the same: corporate sponsorship of government. Anything goes when it comes to corporate fundraising. Interestingly, many of these corporate donors like to play it safe with a winner on each team, therefore making hefty donations to both Republicans and Democrats. These corporations do not finance these elected officials because they are nice patriotic people. They expect something in return: legislation favorable to their own interests. Most often, however, these interests do not align with those of the American people whom our elected officials are supposed to represent. The act of quasi-official government agencies supporting one or both parties conceptually has no integrity and is unworthy of a democracy.

---

[199] Mann/Ornstein, *ante*, p. 71.

The current gridlock in government is the result of conservative politics reinforced by the influence of big money - by lobbying. The process has fundamentally changed the nation. Robert Kaiser's book, *So Damn Much Money: The Triumph of Lobbying and the Corrosion of the American Government,* is an epic piece.[200] He explains that candidates spend an excessive amount of time raising funds and that U.S. elections are drowning in money. Campaign funding has become a normal, if not substantial, part of lobbying. The financial outlay per candidate and the total sum spent have increased explosively since 2008. The press reports that elected members of Congress use half their time funding their re-elections.[201] Indirect and direct corruption benefits from this. Mann and Ornstein state that wealth has long played a problematic role in American democracy: "Reconciling the tension between economic inequality and political equality, while preserving the constitutional guarantee of free speech, is no easy task."[202]

Members of Congress work in large office buildings on either side of the Capitol. Lobbyists are said to have free access to them. Inquiries and appeals concerning any imaginable subject are deposited on lawmakers' desks; lobbyists hand out presents and information and garnish campaign funds with money. These activities have been observed critically since the beginning of American democracy. Occasionally, lobbyists' activities are conspicuous and relevant legislation is applied. Jack Abramoff

---

[200] Robert G. Kaiser, *So Much Damn Money: The Triumph of Lobbying and the Corrosion of American Government* (New York: Vintage Books, 2009), quoted in Mann/Ornstein, *ante,* p. 67.

[201] Tim Roemer, "Why do Congressmen spend only half of their time serving us?" *Newsweek,* July 29, 2015. Or: Ryan Grimm and Sabrina Siddiqui, "Call Time for Congress Shows how Fundraising Dominates Bleak Work Life," *The Huffington Post,* January 8, 2013.

[202] Mann/Ornstein, *ante,* p. 69.

was convicted in 2006 for his work as a lobbyist and for offering lobbying jobs to members of Congress once their terms were finished.[203] In return, he and his team expected legislative work favoring their cause.

Unfortunately, this is not an uncommon occurrence in politics; it happens every day.

Members of Congress and lobbyists seem to think alike. Close ties developed over many visits turn into friendships. Lines blur. In the end, it becomes more and more difficult to discern between what is an informal exchange and where actual lobbying begins. Furthermore, the careers of retired members of Congress often naturally continue in the world of lobbying. These people have sufficient contacts with former colleagues, who serve their new concerns. Comments made by advisors during elected officials' terms as senators and representatives often hint that future employment on the "other side" is possible.[204]

Former Republican Congressman Newt Gingrich's network of companies and influential groups was referred to as "Newt, Inc." Even after he retired, contributions not designated for any specific purpose continued to flow into the "Newt, Inc." account. According to Mann and Ornstein, the government-financed Federal Home Loan Mortgage Corporation, a.k.a. Freddie Mac, was among Gingrich's contributors.[205] According to Sean McElwee, writing for *Salon*, in 1980, the highest contribution was $1.72 million. In 2012, this sum rose to $56.8 million, which is 33 times the initial amount.[206]

---

[203] Mann/Ornstein, *ante*, p. 68.
[204] Mann/Ornstein, *ante*, p. 69.
[205] Mann/Ornstein, *ante*, p. 69.
[206] Sean McElwee, "The great American rip-off: How big-money corruption fuels racial inequality," *Salon*, December 21, 2014.

It should come as no surprise that companies making immense campaign contributions are more likely to receive government contracts. Researcher Christopher Witco wrote that such companies have better or direct access to members of Congress in order to influence legislation or decisions concerning urgent political issues.[207] Once again, it becomes all too apparent that it is all about gaining influence on political decisions that favor one's personal business and interests. This is a form of corruption.

Fundamental changes in campaign and party financing regulations are essential in order to reduce polarization between Republicans and Democrats. According to Mann and Ornstein, this must be a joint effort: the IRS needs to intervene, as does the Federal Election Commission, which is in charge of Congressional elections and which needs to provide clear rules. Furthermore, the Federal Communications Commission (FCC) needs to attend to its duties and provide donor identification, while the Securities and Exchange Commission (SEC) must closely monitor quarterly and annual reports.[208]

The Federal Election Commission (FEC), in particular, should play a leading role in the nation's voting process. *Should,* however, is a far cry from *does;* reality paints a different picture. Ignoring FEC's concerns is the result of years of unilateral interference by the Republican Party. "The leader of the Republican Senate Majority, Senator McConnell, is really the whole key to the FEC," wrote Andy Kroll in a 2011 piece for *Mother Jones.* "He realized several years ago that a very effective

---

[207] Christopher Witko, "Campaign Contributions, Access and Government Contracting." *Oxford Journals, The Journal of Public Administration Research and Theory 21(4).* 2011.
[208] Mann/Ornstein, *ante,* pp. 152-160.

way to minimize the effect of federal laws is to undermine the regulator."[209]

Is that a sign of a distorted democracy?

For decades, America has served as a beacon of democracy. Unfortunately, the principles of democracy have eroded slowly and over time. Mostly small, formal aspects of an otherwise lively democracy have been changed during the past three decades and this in turn has *changed the character of the U.S. democracy.*

Party politics have become bickering performances on television's grand stage. There is a lack of action in favor of the country's wellbeing. Politicians are on a troubled, self-fulfilling path to accommodate the wealthy. Party lines are placed ahead of the country's welfare and its many problems. In many states, the will of voters can be grossly distorted, if not falsified. Election procedures in 47 states are not regulated democratically. They can be likened to a ship with unsecured cargo: with each wave, the chaos ensuing from the boat's rolling and pitching gets worse. The cargo shifts, and the vessel's equilibrium is compromised. It is a difficult feat to find balance again.

I am frequently reminded that the America is a young nation, but that seems like an empty excuse considering that the country's history is over 200 years old. This excuse conceals the blatant deficiencies, such as gerrymandering or other undemocratic conducts and attitudes. The American citizen is well aware of these deficiencies, but has neither the will nor the opportunity to make improvements other than by voting—and many times, as noted before, not even that is possible.

---

[209] Andy Kroll, "What the FEC?" *Mother Jones,* April 18, 2011, quoted in Mann/Ornstein, *ante,* p. 154.

Sports vs. Politics

Even our sporting events are not immune from political influence; were you aware that the U.S. military paid $10.4 million to the NFL for patriotic displays and tributes to the troops?[210] Altogether, according to this McCain/Flake report, the Department of Defense invests $53 million to all sporting events combined. You can say that even our patriotism is influenced with dollars.[211] But the American love of sports shows another, oft-overlooked aspect of American culture and thought: our tendency to shy away from unpleasant topics which we feel we have no control over.

In a 2014 interview in *AlterNet*, American historian and cognitive scientist Noam Chomsky expressed his fascination regarding how so many Americans talk about the details of sports on call-in radio shows, displaying that their knowledge on the matter is vast and their analysis runs deep. They can express themselves confidently and have strong opinions about team decisions. These analytical skills, however, fall short once the discussion switches to local political or international issues. Chomsky suggests that people feel powerless to influence local, national, or international events. They apply their general knowledge and intellectual skills to subjects with which they feel comfortable and they tend to avoid problems which they believe they have no influence over because the decision-making power lies elsewhere.

---

[210] Dave Hogg, "The Military Paid Pro Sports Teams 10.4 Million For Patriotic Displays, Troop tributes," *SBNation*, November 4, 2015 (The McCain/Flake Report). https://www.sbnation.com/2015/11/4/9670302/nfl-paid-patriotism-troops-mcain-flake-report-million

[211] Hogg, Ibid.

Chomsky added:

"Now it seems to me that the same intellectual skills and capacity for understanding and for accumulating evidence and gaining information and thinking through problems could be used—would be used—under different systems of governance, which involve popular participation in important decision-making, in areas that really matter to human life."[212]

He continued by explaining that people live in two different worlds: one is close and identifiable (e.g. the world of sports), while the other is far away and unreachable (e.g. the political outcomes in Washington). The general public seems to feel helpless when it comes to political decision-making. What Chomsky is saying here is that if Americans transferred the same deep analytical thought that they use with sports and applied it the same way to issues that are more life-altering and important—such as politics and social issues—then we could reshape America in a profound way.

Americans today pride themselves on being better informed than generations past. But most research contradicts that notion by indicating that in reality, Americans are growing even less informed. Although, independent print media, the readership has declined so much in recent years that few are even exposed to it. Cable and internet news which has evolved into the primary news source is partisan entertainment under the guise of real journalism.

Which begs the question: are people being kept away from politics on purpose? It would seem by choice, that Americans are flocking to these unreliable news outlets because rather than a

---

[212] Chomsky, "Why people know ..", *ante.*

quality, reliable source they are seeking only a cheerleader to reinforce their own internalized political beliefs.

The American Voting Paradox: Choosing the Right Party

Living in the United States is a very pleasant experience for many people. With the right amount of money, an infinite number of products and services are at your disposal. On the other hand, daily politics are full of contradictions and surprises.

I am pointing to two articles here. The first is an excerpt from the November 20th, 2014 edition of MSNBC's Rachel Maddow Show, a progressive, daily political news program. The second is an article published in *Salon* magazine by Edwin Lyngar, a conservative American, formerly of the GOP, who became a potential supporter of former Democratic presidential nominee Hillary Clinton. Examining these reports reveals that political concerns and personal actions of individuals are often contradictory.

Following the 2014 U.S. Congressional election, talk show host Rachel Maddow reported that the results of an NBC/*Wall Street Journal* poll about the voting behavior of the American electorate showed that 57% of those polled approved of immigration reform.[213] 74% approved of President Obama's proposal to allow undocumented, illegal workers to pay a fine, pay taxes, and undergo background checks to receive legal documentation. Interestingly, when asked whether they favored

---

[213] The Rachel Maddow Show on MSNBC, November 20, 2014, and Patrick O'Connor, "Poll Finds Americans Want Parties to Work Together," *The Wall Street Journal*, November 19, 2014.

the actions the President was taking, the majority were clearly against him. This suggests that the electorate approves of concrete measures but did not support President Obama's efforts to act on his proposals.

The Congress has a habit of ignoring important current issues. Maddow cited a list of the top five popular policies that American voters asked Congress to carry out, namely: lowering the cost of student loans, increased spending on infrastructure, raising the Federal minimum wage, spending more to fight the Ebola virus outbreak, and limiting carbon emissions to fight climate change. The poll showed that the electorate was very satisfied with the results of the 2012 election. Interestingly, the majorities in the House of Representatives and the Senate are not in favor of addressing these five topics. "It's almost like people don't really know what's going on in politics. Or, they don't really know what decisions are being made and by whom in Washington," Maddow pointed out.[214]

How can it be that the U.S. electorate chooses—as the largest and determining power in Congress, no less—a party that fights against the main economic and social interests of the nation? How is it that the electorate does not recognize this paradox? How is it that, in retrospect, these people still feel that the party is doing a good job?

Here is Edwin Lyngar's story, demonstrating the voting paradox.

I was a 20-year-old college dropout with no more than $100 in the bank the day my son was born in 1994. I'd been in the Coast Guard just over six months. Joining the service was my solution to a lot of

---

[214] The Rachel Maddow Show, November 20, 2014.

problems, not the least of which was being married to a pregnant, 19-year-old fellow dropout. We were poor, and my overwhelming response to poverty was a profound shame that drove me into the arms of the people least willing to help—conservatives.

Just before our first baby arrived, my wife and I walked into the social services office near the base where I was stationed in rural North Carolina. "You qualify for WIC and food stamps," the middle-aged woman said. I don't know whether she disapproved of us or if all social services workers in the South oozed an understated unpleasantness. We took the Women, Infants, Children Vouchers for free peanut butter, cheese and baby formula and got into the food stamp line.

Looking around, I saw no other young servicemen. Coming from the white working class, I'd always been taught that food stamps were for the "others"—failures, drug addicts, or immigrants, maybe—not for real Americans like me. I could not bear the stigma, so we walked out before our number was called.

Even though we didn't take the food stamps, we lived in the warm embrace of the federal government with subsidized housing and utilities, courtesy of Uncle Sam. Yet I blamed all of my considerable problems on the government, the only institution that was actively working to alleviate my suffering. I railed against government spending (i.e., raising my own salary). At the same time, the earned income tax credit was the only way I could balance my budget at the end of the year.

I felt my own poverty was a moral failure. To support my feelings of inadequacy, every move I made only pushed me deeper into poverty. I bought a car and got screwed on the financing. The credit I could get, I overused and was overpriced to start with. My wife couldn't get or keep a job, and we could not afford reliable day care in any case. I was naive, broke and uneducated but still felt entitled to a middle-class existence.

If you had taken WIC and the EITC away from me, my son would still have eaten, but my life would have been much more miserable. Without government help, I would have had to borrow money from my family more often. I borrowed money from my parents less than a handful of times, but I remember every single instance with a burning shame. To ask for money was to admit defeat, to be a de facto loser.

To make up for my own failures, I voted to give rich people tax cuts, because somewhere deep inside, I knew they were better than me. They earned it. My support for conservative politics was atonement for the original sin of being white trash.

In my second tour of duty, I grew in rank and my circumstances improved. I voted for George W. Bush. I sent his campaign money, even though I had little to spare. During the Bush v. Gore recount, I grabbed a sign and walked the streets of San Francisco to protest, carrying my toddler on my shoulders. I got emotional, thinking of "freedom."

Sometime after he took office, I watched Bush speak at an event. He talked of tax cuts. "It's the people's money," he said. By then I was making even better money, but I didn't care about tax cuts for myself. I was still paying little if any income tax, but I believed in "fairness." The "death tax" (a.k.a. the estate tax) was unfair and rich people paid more taxes so they should get more of a tax break. I ignored my own personal struggles when I made political decisions.

By the financial meltdown of 2008, I was out of the military and living in Reno, Nevada—a state hard hit by the downturn. I voted libertarian that election year, even though the utter failure of the free market was obvious. The financial crisis proved that rich people are no better than me, and in fact, are often inferior to average people. They crash companies, loot pensions and destroy banks, and when they hit a snag, they scream to be rescued by government largess. By contrast, I continued to pay my oversize mortgage for years, even as my home lost more than half its value. I viewed my bad investment as yet another moral failure. When it comes to voting and investing, rich people make calculated decisions, while regular people make "emotional" and "moral" ones. Despite growing self-awareness, I pushed away reality for another election cycle.

In 2010, I couldn't support my own Tea Party candidate for Senate because Sharron Angle was an obvious lunatic. I instead sent money to the Rand Paul campaign. Immediately the Tea Party-led Congress pushed drastic cuts in government spending that prolonged the economic pain. The jobs crisis in my own city was exacerbated by the needless gutting of government employment. The people who crashed the economy—bankers and business people—screamed about government spending and exploited Tea Party outrage to get their own taxes lowered. Just months after the Tea Party victory, I realized my mistake, but I could only watch as the people I supported inflicted massive, unnecessary pain on the economy through government shutdowns, spending cuts and gleeful cruelty.

I finally "got it." In 2012, I shunned my self-destructive voting habits and supported Obama. I only wished there were a major party more liberal than the Democrats for whom I could vote. Even as I saw the folly of my own lifelong voting record, many of my friends and family moved further into the Tea Party embrace, even as conservative policies made their lives worse.

I have a close friend on permanent disability. He votes reliably for the most extreme conservative in every election. Although he's a Nevadan, he lives just across the border in California, because that progressive state provides better social safety nets for its disabled. He always votes for the person most likely to slash the *program he depends on daily for his own survival. It's like clinging to the end of a thin rope and voting for the rope-cutting razor party.*

The people who most support the Republicans and the Tea Party carry a secret burden. Many know that they are one medical emergency or broken down car away from ruin, and they blame the government. They vote against their own interests, often hurting themselves in concrete ways, in a vain attempt to deal with their own, misguided shame about being poor. They believe "freedom" is the answer, even though they live a form of wage indenture in a rigged system.

I didn't become a liberal until I was nearly 40. By the time I came around, I was an educated professional, married to another professional. We're "making it," whatever that means these days. I gladly pay taxes now, but this attitude is also rooted in self-interest. I have relatives who are poor, and without government services, I might have to support them. We can all go back to living in clans, like cavemen, or we can build institutions and programs that help people who need it. It seems like a great bargain to me.

I'm angry at my younger self, not for being poor, but for supporting politicians who would have kept me poor if they were able. Despite my personal attempts to destroy the safety net, those benefits helped me. I earned a bachelor's degree for free courtesy of a federal program, and after my military service I used the GI Bill to get two graduate degrees, all while making ends meet with the earned income tax credit. The GI Bill not only helped me, it also created much of the American middle class after World War II. Conservatives often crow about "supporting the military," but imagine how much better America would be if the government used just 10 percent of the military budget to pay for universal higher education, rather than saddling 20-year-olds with mortgage-like debt.

> *Government often fails because the moneyed interests don't want it to succeed. They hate government and most especially activist government (a.k.a. government that does something useful). Their hatred for government is really disdain for Americans, except as consumers or underpaid labor.*
>
> *Sadly, it took me years—decades—to see the illogic of supporting people who disdain me. But I'm a super-slow learner. I wish I could take the poorest, struggling conservatives and shake them. I would scream that their circumstances or failures or joblessness are not all their fault. They should wise up and vote themselves a break. Rich people vote their self-interest in every single election. Why don't poor people?*
>
> -Edwin Lyngar[215]

This report is straightforward, and every sentence should be underlined. Lyngar is poor and feels emotionally inferior to the upper class. In the American social hierarchy, he classifies himself as if he is at the bottom of the ladder. He is unsuccessful; he has fallen below the poverty line and, therefore, is eligible for many of the country's social programs.

His own economic status is perceived as low and degrading. Voting for the same party as the rich and successful appears to increase his own status and the recognition he seeks. He wants to hide his position as a low-income earner and side with successful people. He is hard-working but can't seem to get ahead and continues to support the party that he believes will improve his lifestyle.

Lyngar suggests that the small, minimally successful middle-class citizen elects the party that represents everything he wants

---

[215] Edwin Lyngar, published in *SALON*, July 16, 2014

to be—rich and living large. In other words, the middle class and the low-income earners vote for their ideal, their dream, thus discriminating against themselves by supporting the rich. This behavior is a classic example of internalized oppression. The rich, on the other hand, naturally support the party that supports them and their interests and improves their situation.

The greed for private wealth is everywhere, and that is the only universally accepted rule in this country. Author and activist Edward Abbey wrote, "We are belabored by the insistence on the part of our politicians, businessmen and military leaders, and the claque of scriveners who serve them, that 'growth' and 'power' are intrinsic goods, of which we can never have enough."[216]

The working poor and those who feel cheated by being left out of the American dream politically ally themselves with the super-rich and the corporations, not realizing that this alliance, if successful, will cement their fate and that of their children. Why do Americans vote against their own social and economic interests? This is a blind spot of many low-income workers. It is a pitfall—and, often, their downfall.

Perhaps the majority of Americans have internalized the values of reckless freedom and emphasis on individual interests, and they do not pay attention to the distortions and oddities that come with it. Eccentric, extremely intricate, and detailed laws are not questioned. Very few people ever achieve the status of the richest 1% of the population—the statistic speaks for itself, after all—but all want to achieve it and believe they can. For too many workers, the "American dream" translates to simply gaining an increase in food stamp benefits rather than obtaining a good

---

[216] Edward Abbey, "Down the River with Henry Thoreau," *Manuscript*. Entry of November 9, 1980.

paying job and rising up the social and economic ladder. Therein lies the perfect veneer to internalize a goal that 99% of Americans will never reach.

Lyngar's younger self—representing countless of other citizens like him— is an image of a lost loner who is not informed. He does not have the facts or the energy to draw the right conclusions. He sabotages his own core values and denies his own needs and social class.

Libertarian Politics

The 1980 Election and the 2016 Republican Agenda

In 1980, the Libertarian Party nominated Ed Clark, a lawyer and Harvard graduate who had vied for the position of Governor of California in 1978, as their party's candidate. The vice-presidential candidate was lawyer and TV personality David Koch who, along with his brother, Charles, is today a major contributor to the Republican Party.

This was the 1980 Libertarian platform:

- "We urge the repeal of federal campaign finance laws, and the immediate abolition of the despotic Federal Election Commission."
- "We favor the abolition of Medicare and Medicaid programs."
- "We favor the repeal of the fraudulent, virtually bankrupt, and increasingly oppressive Social Security system.

Pending that repeal, participation in Social Security should be made voluntary."

- "We oppose all personal and corporate income taxation, including capital gains taxes."
- "We support the eventual repeal of all taxation."
- "We support repeal of all laws which impede the ability of any person to find employment, such as minimum wage laws."
- "We advocate the complete separation of Education and State. Government schools lead to the indoctrination of children and interfere with the free choice of individuals. Government ownership, operation, regulation, and subsidy of schools and colleges should be ended."
- "We support the abolition of the Environmental Protection Agency."
- "We demand the return of America's railroad system to private ownership. We call for the privatization of the public roads and national highway system."
- "We oppose all government welfare, relief projects, and 'aid to the poor' programs. All these government programs are privacy-invading, paternalistic, demeaning, and inefficient. The proper source of help for such persons is the voluntary efforts of private groups and individuals."[217]

This platform emerged as the brain child and agenda of the wealthy Koch brothers. Contrary to popular Libertarian myth, this platform makes no mention nor offers any actual protection or hope for struggling working people. After 35 years, these Libertarian principals are still the same. The first item on the list

[217] Senator Bernie Sanders, "What do the Koch Brothers Want?" http://www.sanders.senate.gov/koch-brothers [consulted May 8, 2015].

became a reality in 2010, with the U.S. Supreme Court's decision regarding Citizens United. The privatization of railways, however, was only a half-hearted effort.[218] The National Railroad Passenger Corporation, known as Amtrak, is arguably a corporation, but it is owned by the government.

The above list of the libertarian agenda reflects the development of the Republican Party, which has adopted these ideas over the last few years. It is safe to say that the Koch brothers are responsible for this reorientation. Vermont Senator Bernie Sanders, the progressive 2016 Democratic presidential candidate, said: "What is extraordinary about this document, the 1980 Libertarian Party platform, is that what was considered 'extremist' and 'kooky' in 1980 has become part of today's mainstream Republican thinking." [219]

In other words, the Koch brothers have been enormously successful in moving the agenda of the Republican Party far to the right under the guise of Libertarianism. Regardless of how they market themselves to voters, the truth of the agenda parallels the Libertarian intention, which decrees there will only be a few super-rich citizens, a small middle class and many working poor. This is hardly a winning strategy to garner large support among hard-working American voters, and yet it does, playing on a skewed psychology. The latter dream of a life in the upper class and, therefore, will support their opponents and inadvertently punish themselves ...

In the 2016 presidential election, the fundamental Libertarian objectives permeated the Republican platform like never before. In the 114th and 115th legislative sessions (2015-2018), both chambers of Congress have a Republican majority. A

---

[218] Tad deHaven, "Privatizing Amtrak," Cato Institute, Downsizing the Federal Government, June 2010.
[219] Senator Bernie Sanders, *ante*.

budget draft reflecting Libertarian values was adopted in March 2015 by both chambers of Congress.[220] Now with a Republican president having been inaugurated in January 2017, one can assume that the final budget will be adopted with the following priorities.

"Politics is the gentle art of getting votes from the poor and campaign funds from the rich, by promising to protect each from the other."

-Oscar Ameringer, 1870–1943

In such a scenario, major budget cuts would adversely affect social security legislation. The health insurance mandate of the Affordable Health Care Act of 2010 would be abolished, and many Medicare services would be greatly reduced.[221] The arduous and Herculean task of insuring more Americans' health would plummet from any level of progress it may have currently reached. Health insurance companies would remain private. Federal laws defining minimum services as well as all 200 social programs would be abolished.

The pension system would not have any improvements. If today's Republicans had their way, they would abolish Social Security completely.[222] The Republican Party does not support the food stamp program and would love to cut this $300 billion Federally-funded program from the budget. The state of Kansas

---

[220] David Espo and Andrew Taylor, "House, Senate panels adopt tough balanced-budget plans," *Aspen Daily News,* March 20, 2015.

[221] Steven Rosenfeld, "12 Ways the GOP Would Destroy the Country If They Controlled Washington after 2016," *AlterNet,* May 8, 2015.

[222] Rosenfeld, *Ibid.*

has already implemented the GOP's stance on federal programs for the poor and needy: cash payouts are limited to $25 and are coupled with provisions for compulsory work, shopping restrictions, and audits.[223] This can lead to bank fees for those affected, making it nearly impossible to escape the poverty trap. Budget reductions would affect public schools and educational programs as well as state universities and colleges.

Wage earners have been paying into Social Security and Medicare for 40 years in order to have government-regulated health insurance when they retire. A health insurance program, backed by the federal government, in which every hardworking and *not* super-rich American could deeply appreciate, is a good thing. This was something advocated intensively by Bernie Sanders, who wanted to extend Medicare to all ages, thus making the Affordable Health Care Act obsolete.

Instead, another vision for America is brewing in the horizon. You do not have to believe this author's forecast, but the direction that we are heading towards is crystal clear: the road is calling for a significant reduction of all social benefits and a generous increase in military spending. President Trump has already expanded the latter quickly and significantly, ballooning military spending to over $613 billion.[224]

The United States continues to feed its sizeable budget for policing the world. Rosenfeld wrote that the 2015-2016 Federal Budget has already allowed for an additional $187 billion "for unrelated defense needs" abroad.[225] At the same time, funding has been cut for returning war veterans. The U.S. is ready to

---

[223] Tyler Durden, "Broke Kansas To Tax Poor People By Placing $25 Limit on ATM Withdrawals," *Zero Hedge,* May 25, 2015.

[224] Michael D. Shear, "Touring Warship, Trump Pushes Plan to Expand Military," *The New York Times,"* March 2, 2017.

[225] Rosenfeld, *ante.*

strike abroad, yet those who are actually doing the fighting are not cared for with the attention that they deserve on the home front. The problems at home have gotten so serious that Veterans Affairs Secretary Eric Shinseki resigned in 2014, taking responsibility for problems such as long wait times for patients in VA facilities and false record-keeping by his agency.[226]

The Influence of Libertarianism

Libertarianism is U.S. conservatism in its most extreme and pure form. While Republicans would like to reduce social programs, Libertarians like Senator Rand Paul would like to eliminate them altogether. They would, if they could, happily eliminate vital federal programs and regulations, and strip or eliminate entire departments. Libertarians basically uphold such a limited federal role that their worldview essentially translates to a dog-eat-dog society.

The Libertarian ideology in America has grown in acceptance over the last two decades. Beginning around 2007, the rise of the Tea Party influenced the Republican Party's shift to the right with emphasis on Libertarian values, such as lower taxes and smaller government. The Tea Party movement, founded in 1971, is not an official political party; its influence has been indirectly felt through the Republican Party. Presently, the movement's popularity is waning; according to a 2014 *New York Times* report, only 8% of the population still embraces this political thought.[227] The Republican Party, however, has adopted much of

---

[226] Katie Zezima, "Everything you need to know about the VA—and the scandals engulfing it," *The Washington Post*, May 30, 2014.

[227] Allison Kopicki, "Support Is Thin for Tea Party, but It Retains Its Muscles," *The New York Times,* June 24, 2014.

the Libertarian ideology, suggesting that the movement is no longer necessary as its values have already infiltrated one of the two largest and most significant political parties in the nation.

The same goes for the Libertarian Party; just as it has absorbed Tea Party ideologies the Republican Party has absorbed both Tea Party and Libertarian values. Since 2008, emphasis on individual responsibility, rejection of government social support programs, support of lower taxes, and tax breaks for the rich have all gained more popularity within the party.

The linked concepts of liberal and conservative are a reality for Democrats and Republicans. In America, a "liberal" is a social democrat who understands the civil liberties of a modern state, such as freedom of speech, press, and religion, as well as equal treatment before the law. A traditional political liberal approves of the separation of church and state, universal suffrage, civil rights, environmental-protection, healthcare, equal education opportunities, and an effective transportation infrastructure.

One could assume that a political conservative rejects all of the above, preferring instead a sleek, strong government with fewer taxes, little regulation, free enterprise, and a national military. They indeed argue that social programs are the responsibility of religious and voluntary welfare organizations. Conservatives believe that the government cannot solve society's problems, especially poverty and inequality. They fear that government programs foster dependency on government agencies and reduce individual responsibilities; they argue that supportive measures for individuals favor certain social classes or groups. The citizens' security, liberties, and the protection of private property are their core concerns. Welfare is not their priority and they reject the notion that the government has a responsibility for other citizens' welfare.

Followers of the Libertarian ideology are very critical of any government action, demanding the elimination of government involvement in education, environmental protection, and social legislation. They suggest that government involvement in these areas be turned over to the private sector. They would like to abolish the Internal Revenue Service. They do, however, support the Armed Forces. Their concern is to protect private property and entrepreneurial rights. While Libertarians tout their support for the constitutional rights of all Americans, their policies and proposals indicate otherwise. Instead of protecting the rights of everyday people, the Libertarians strive only to protect the rights of corporations and the wealthy.

Ayn Rand and the Philosophical Principle of Libertarianism

You cannot even bring up the right-wing in this country without mentioning the influence of philosopher and author Ayn Rand. Born in Russia in 1905, Rand's view quickly structured conservative viewpoints and an idealistic view of capitalism.[228] The Libertarian tradition of thought is not solely based on a foundation of economics. The attitude that one can best achieve happiness and satisfaction solely through one's own efforts is based on a philosophical principle. The alleged objectivist philosophy is presented in the literary works of Ayn Rand.

Ayn Rand emigrated to the U.S. from the Soviet Union in 1926. Because of her experiences within the communist system, she was only able to see the positive sides of capitalism with its emphasis on individual freedom. Here, in the "Land of

---

[228] https://www.biography.com/people/ayn-rand-9451526

Opportunity," she became a proponent of free-market economics and campaigned for the anti-communist movement. She published, among other things, two very successful novels in which she developed her theory of Objectivism.

The Fountainhead (1943) is a novel about connections and relationships in the world of architects and publishers. In that world, Rand set forth the competition for contracts and the interconnected intrigues and influence dramas that play out on different levels. The honest protagonist prevails alone against all the profiteers and second-rate figures described in the book's different networks of influence. Everything turns out all right in the battle of an individual genius against the collective powers surrounding him.

Her other book, *Atlas Shrugged* (1957), is a story about the American business world that was set in a not-so-distant future. Wealthy capitalists and scions of big family companies, as well as engineers and architects, go on strike and let their companies fail or be sold. Radical regulations, imposed on business by the government, are the principal reasons for their rejection. The capitalists disappear without a trace and are soon joined by scientists and artists in their mountain retreat, where they found a new, free economy.

In the strike declaration and through the book's protagonist, John Galt, Ayn Rand presented a new philosophy: Objectivism. The strike enacted by the representatives of a prosperous business world clearly described Rand's idea that the commitment of these people is indispensable to the well-being of the entire country. The proponents of the strike wished to rebuild the failing country into a society that would be in accordance with their principles, and they ultimately founded exactly such a society.

According to Objectivism, all knowledge and life experiences are based on sensory perception and reason.[229] For Rand, experiences were considered as objective facts; her philosophy was based on the principle that an objective truth exists independently of the observer. There are values that are objective in an absolute sense. The absolute, objective truth can be recognized by normal reason, and internalized. The principles of Objectivism state that only the individual's own ideas and ideals are valid. A central organ for seeking and communicating the truth, such as the entity of the church in the Middle Ages, does not exist. Nor are there feelings, instinct, and revelations; Rand rejected these as source of knowledge. According to Rand's view, any *a priori* (i.e., deduced by reasoning from self-evident propositions) understandings, such as in the sense of spiritual epiphanies cannot exist; only the immediate impression has objective validity.[230]

Rand did not explain the source of the "power of reason" that apparently guides the individual. Because this power is given to the reasonable person—instead of being cultivated, for instance—it appears that this reasoning itself must be regarded as an *a priori* understanding, which seems like a paradox. In any case, this "power of reason" is not a subject clarified thoroughly by Rand. As a newcomer to this philosophical world, the reader remains lost, not knowing which "reason" he or she should find or absorb in order to experience the realization of the Objectivist philosophy.

Furthermore, within the Objectivist ethical system, the individual is supposed only let himself or herself be motivated by personal interests. This rational and ethical selfishness is meant

---

[229] Wikipedia, "Objectivism by Ayn Rand" [consulted November 9, 2015]. https://en.wikipedia.org/wiki/Objectivism_(Ayn_Rand).
[230] Wikipedia, *Ibid.*

to provide the basis for a happy life. Selflessness and consideration of others' interests—according to this theory—would prevent the realization of a humanistic lifestyle and would stand in the way of personal happiness.

Using this principle as a first stepping stone, it does not require a big leap to reach the viewpoint of emphasizing the rights of the individual in political philosophy, especially property rights, and to see "laissez-faire capitalism" as the only moral authority. In this manner, total economic freedom goes hand-in-hand with business, and government has no legitimate authority to regulate it in any way. The activities of the government are limited to "the police, to protect you from criminals; the army, to protect you from foreign conquest; and the courts, to protect your property and contracts."[231]

This way of thinking has nothing but contempt for systems like absolute monarchy, theocracy, communism, Nazism, anarchism, dictatorship, and democratic socialism. Normally, Objectivism is classified as conservative or Libertarian. Rand herself was not happy with this description; she called her philosophy "radical capitalism."

The central demands of Libertarians focus on the happiness of the individual without consideration for others, and without any help from the social community. Libertarianism is the ultimate personification of selfishness; it is a fully "what's-in-it-for me" mentality with little to no concern for the larger society or the greater good. In this scenario, businessmen become the central figures in the production of goods and services. Apparently and incredulously, it appears this is all the individual needs to achieve happiness.

---

[231] Ayn Rand, *The Virtue of Selfishness* (New York: New American Library, 1964), p 109. [The cited tasks of government are mentioned as well in other works; the selection of this book is coincidental.]

Zeit Online journalist Felix Stephan points out: "The despotic business leaders are, in Rand's world, the truly inspired men. Only they have the strength to forgive; only they can experience the full potential of love and only they have the courage to fight back against a tyrannical, hypocritical world. They are civilized, reasonable, curious, romantic, and gallant."[232] He goes on to illustrate how the contribution made by businessmen to the general wellbeing of society is emphasized with ideals, and that the most praiseworthy deeds of humanity are attributed to this group. Only individual deeds exist, and the best characteristics are attributed to businessmen; as Stephan explains:

> "The roles are clearly defined: the hardworking, visionary, good guys work only for their own benefit, and thereby inevitably for the well-being of the nation and the world. The bad guys in the shadows plunder the profits in the name of the common good, with the purpose of creating a communist dictatorship. There is no grey zone between these two extremes; everyone is either on one side or on the other. At best, they are able to recognize the error of their ways and cross over to the side of the capitalists. The apologists of the common good, morals and metaphysics, on the other hand, are grotesquely overdrawn weaklings: they steal, rape, betray, lie, and give orders."[233]

Libertarianism adopted many promises of Objectivism, including the idea that the individual should only pay attention to his own selfish interests. I say that every human being has a justifiable responsibility for his own well-being first. That said, our individual lives are not the "be all, end all" of the world. We

---

[232] Felix Stephan, "Puppenhausprosa der Kapitalisten" ("Dollhouse prose of Capitalists"), *Die ZEIT (ZEITonline)*, August 17, 2012.
[233] Stephan, *Ibid.*

live in various communities and do have a responsibility to contribute to these communities. And yet, there is no acknowledgment of our communities in Libertarianism: there is only the well-being of the individual. This makes no sense, as our interactions and collective successes would be *nothing* without the contributions of our communities. The greatest contributions to the development of social media, for example, came from a combination of publicly-financed research and the contributions of individual engineers. While the individual contribution is recognized, we must also acknowledge the contributions of other communities, including taxpayer and private trusts.

Entrepreneurial activities may not lead to the well-being of communities *per se*. Successful industrial businesses do have the additional responsibility to share in the resolution of environmental problems, maintaining infrastructure and improving education. Entrepreneurial activities are just a link in the total economic chain. The individual is invisible. As a result, businesses must be seen in a larger context.

Nothing sustainable is ever achieved in society without collective effort. Americans will rapidly adapt to almost every condition or product, and corporations prey upon this weakness. The prevalence of plastic is an example of this. At first, consumers loved plastic, finding it useful and convenient, but the long-term negative ramifications of the product were never even considered. It did not take long before the disposing of plastic waste became a problem. Burning it produced poisonous residues. Dumping it in landfills turned out to be a bad idea, since some plastic is not biodegradable. Even the manufacturing of plastic is toxic to people and the environment. The disposal of plastic became more complicated than its production. Regulations for the use and disposal of primary products had to be established—and this became a community effort.

The success of Rand's books, and the significant response from her influenced readership, cannot only be attributed to the author's skills; her work found a solid market when it captured the hearts of Libertarians. Why was *Atlas Shrugged,* with its self-centered thoughts and ideals, so well received? The author promoted the creation of quick success based on material wealth, at the cost of the community. It appealed to people who promoted and lived by these same values. It also promoted the notion that a person with materialistic success—a more expensive car, for example, or a bigger house—must automatically be a better and smarter person, and, thus, people think that this sort of person deserves greater respect and should just be held in higher esteem.

Libertarianism idealistically assumes that everyone will automatically do the right thing. Reality is different, however, and if business was voluntarily operating environmentally and socially responsible, there wouldn't be the need for local, state or federal regulations.

People in the corporate world do not do the ideal thing, they do the profitable thing—and often at the expense of the larger community. The result is a need for regulations that have the power and willingness to govern what the corporations can and cannot do. We have these regulations because greed is an attitude and a vice that does not care about the health of the community.

Eric Fromm described the "need a bigger car" situation in his book, *To Have or to Be.*[234] "To have" is in reference to material possessions and the manifestation of power, greed, avarice, and violence. Its opposite is "to be," which is an expression of self-awareness, love, and participation in the community. The role

---

[234] Erich Fromm, *To Have or to Be?* (New York: Harper & Row, 1976).

model of the Libertarian is "to have"; the person's focus is to gain *for the self.* If you are not "the self"—if it is not in the Libertarian's personal interests to help *you*—then you are not going to be included in their strategies for success.

This, it seems to me, begs the question: if you have not yet found the means to achieve your dream of material success, is siding with successful people going to get you there?

What Happened to Genuine Conservatism?

A vibrant democracy requires an adequate representation of different opinions in the public debate, including those of political parties based on the cultural traditions of the country. A democracy is meant to embody a fusion of ideas and philosophies; it is an open conversation that tolerates and considers other viewpoints before automatically rejecting them. It is about uniting people, and creating a sense of belonging in order to empower the country as a strong and sustainable nation.

The U.S. has been politically representative of two distinct and separate ideologies—the liberal and the conservative—since the nation's beginning. There have been periods where one ideology disproportionately influenced the major political parties, one way or another. During the 1960s, for example, the mood of the American majority was moving in a more liberal direction. This resulted in a blurred ideological line between the parties as the trend of American views and lifestyles had shifted to face towards a more liberal direction. Consequently, the Republicans in Congress were just as in favor of the Civil Rights Act or the Voting Act as were the Democrats.

And as a result of this more united, liberal viewpoint of the nation, President Johnson was able to introduce and pass sweeping social legislation with broad bipartisan support. This era was so progressive that even Richard Nixon is said to have been more liberal than any elected Democrat today. The country was so liberal, you can argue, that the conservative viewpoint was not adequately represented.

In every historic case, events occur that begin to swing the pendulum back toward the center and an ideological balance is restored. In this case, the pendulum began to swing in a more conservative direction in the years that followed. The ideas of Barry Goldwater, Milton Friedman, Lewis Powell, James Buchanan, William F. Buckley, and other such politicians and publicists influenced the mainstream thinking of the Republican Party. The result has been an extreme form of conservatism that favors individualism and neglects any form of common responsibility.

Where, perhaps you will ask, can we find genuine conservatism in this country? Conservatism has, over the years, taken on many different forms in many different places. Gregory Schneider wrote that American conservatives "defended ordered liberty [...and] have also sought to preserve the rule of law and the Christian religion. In the twentieth century, they have defended Western civilization from the challenges of modernist culture and totalitarian governments."[235] These values are easy to defend with fair, reasonable arguments. Everyone understands the idea of a small government. The Judeo-Christian worldview and the defense of Western civilization go together, with a pronounced emphasis on freedom, respect for the market

---

[235] Gregory L. Schneider, *The Conservative Century: From Reaction to Revolution* (New York: Rowman & Littlefield, 2009), p. xii.

economy, and a demand for fewer regulations. The commitment to family values is admirable. Yet it is challenging to promote conservative values without falling into the trap of moralizing or limiting the rights of the individual.

The presence of traditional values on the political stage is welcome and so are liberal ideas. In the middle of the 20th century, when the Democratic and Republican parties were comprised of liberals and conservatives, they, together, supported conservative and liberal causes. This blend of political values and ideas made it possible to form bipartisan coalitions and create solutions from compromise. Progress is about finding a compro-mise based on a fusion of tried-and-true beliefs of the past and modern ideas that create new needs. We have done it in the past, as a nation, and we should be able to do it again.

Arthur C. Brooks, of the American Enterprise Institute, is convinced that enforcing and implementing conservative policy is a monumental task.[236] He follows a strict, party-minded line, declaring: "Billions of souls around the world have been able to pull themselves out of poverty thanks to five incredible innovations: globalization, free trade, property rights, the rule of law, and entrepreneurship."[237] This argument is now being embodied worldwide, thanks to America's global diplomatic and military presence. The American ideas of free enterprise and global leadership have enabled progress, which, Brooks said, "has been America's gift to the world."[238] He also calls capitalism "a miracle [treated] like a state secret." Brooks claims that Americans, especially conservatives, are not materialists; instead they are interested in an economically well-functioning policy

---

[236] Arthur C. Brooks, "The Conservative Heart" (brochure), *The American Enterprise Institute*, 2015.
[237] Brooks, *Ibid.,* p. 3.
[238] Brooks, *Ibid.,* p. 4.

with moral righteousness. Yet, he gives no proof of these statements. These remain idealistic and theoretical views in favor of his party and their supporters. His proposals are outdated, covering up the real problems, and, thus, making it difficult, if not impossible, to find solutions to current issues.

Blaming President Obama for poverty in the United States, for example, fits in with the Conservative agenda, but this argument is insufficient. Brooks admits that Republicans have neglected the poor and the poverty-stricken for decades. In his book, he did not address in any way whether, and how, the party's original values could be reintroduced. Brooks maintains that the conservative ideology is not presented well to the American public and is neither the true conservative agenda nor the conservative spirit. He called it a "Conservative Paradox."[239] Brooks yearns for a broad movement that will unite the nation with opportunities for advancement, promotion, and progress for everyone. Its credo should include compassion and fairness, the very essence of the conservative heart. Conservatives should focus on their values;[240] Brooks said that only conservatism stands for real hope, returning strength and power to ordinary people.

In his book, he quoted Friedrich Hayek and former President Ronald Reagan as saying that, "the social safety net for the truly needy people is a major achievement of modern civilization."[241] A major reason for the advocacy of limited government and fiscal conservatism is the fight against tax waste for unneeded services. This is the essence and origin of fiscal conservatism.

But if conservatives are so concerned about the welfare of their fellow "truly needy" and "ordinary" people, why are they

---

[239] Brooks, *Ibid.*, p. 12.
[240] Brooks, *Ibid.*, p. 20.
[241] Brooks, *Ibid.*, p. 23.

stooping so low in their game of political warfare? Gerry-mandering, and the restrictions of voting rights, does not support the democratic spirit. Republican statements toward fellow citizens are contemptuous only because those citizens express another political viewpoint. To perform and win popularity, the party is using tricks and odd tactics. The examples mentioned in this book, about obstacles set up against American democracy, are mainly associated with the Republican Party. The Republican Party is in crisis, and so is the two party system, including the Democratic Party. And the American democracy is in turmoil.

Why, I wonder, is American conservatism aggressive and evangelical? Is it because conservatism has so little to offer the American people that it has to resort to tricks or lies in order to garnish any support of it all?

As an economist, I declare that American involvement in Vietnam, Iraq, and Afghanistan has sabotaged the world's image of American democracy. It is naïve to think that capitalism can fight poverty on a national or global scale. If legislation in the Motherland of Democracy creates lasting poverty, the role model of America's shining democracy loses its promise. I say that the U.S. market economy needs additional social legislation to ensure social justice.

America must face long-ignored demands and make decisive changes to archaic structures and legislation. Successful and sustainable solutions of social legislation can be found in well-rated democracies of other nations, but not in our nation's Republican Party. Democracy is more than just legal compliance; democracy is meant to serve the common good. Adopting a majority decision or making a compromise, even if it does not meet party ideals, is crucial for democracy.

Part 5: American Democracy Unveiled

A Strategic Approach to Legal Principles and Legislation

According to American business strategy organizations, U.S. law, based on the Anglican approach of its Founding Fathers, complies with "common law" principles. Contracts mention all details, they cover all outcomes; therefore, they are usually very long. Even simple purchase agreements contain excerpts from legal texts, explaining detailed rules.

U.S. legislation is comprehensive and follows the same rules of "common law", describing all possible details. The legislative text of the 2010 Patient Protection and Affordable Care Act, for example, is 906 pages long. I doubt if that favors a general overview of problem areas. Exceptions in legislation in favor of a state to please a Senator are said to be common. In this voluminous thicket of legislation there is room for particularities. Loopholes in favor of special interests undermine equality. To reach a goal, two different approaches can be identified: the covert strategy or the open strategy.

Let me explain.

By covert strategy, I mean that stakeholders accept the existing laws, but their actions violate those laws. A prime example of this approach is the Mafia in southern Italy, which pursues its objectives illegally and violently. Its representatives forge contracts with the intention of delivering or performing something quite different than what the contracts stipulate. Some signed contracts for waste disposal in Italy, for example, are not concerned with proper waste management. Consequently, writes Italian journalist Robert Saviano, the waste is dumped in remote valleys in southern Italy and left to rot.[242] Law enforcement officials or private citizens who blow the whistle on these operations become targets. Covert infringement of the law is just as much a crime as overt infringement. Either way, the law is clearly violated.

Saviano is not the first to describe the illegal activities of this secret organization operating under the laws of *omertà*, a term of the Italian mafia that refers to a code of silencing regarding criminal activity and a refusal of handing over respective evidence—a "code of honor", so to speak, in the name of protecting the community. In his book *Gomorrah: A Personal Journey into the Realm of the Camorra*,[243] Saviano wrote that international organizations engaged in illegal activities are a close-knit community existing to avoid social contributions and taxes. Saviano has drawn from various examples to show that it comes down to a network of illegal actions and cover-ups. It is difficult to find the perpetrators when every trail disappears without a trace. Fraud and murder are therefore allowed to

---

[242] Roberto Saviano, *Gomorrah: A Personal Journey into the Violent International Empire of Naples' Organized Crime System* (New York: Picador/Farrar, Straus, Giroux, 2008).
[243] Saviano, *Ibid.*

permeate every aspect of daily life and shape the entire social system, becoming the norm.

In America, Mafia-like behavior is largely unacceptable. Most Americans like to do things correctly according to the law. Yet American democracy, in its current form, provides backdoor opportunities to mold the law to fit certain individual needs. Lobbying evolved to accommodate the demands of specific industries, or groups of people, and to do so by influencing legislation. The only prerequisite is having enough money—i.e. power—to influence Congress.

> "Teach a person their rights and you will have rebellion.
> Teach them their responsibility and you will have revival."
>
> -Cheryl L. Godfrey

How have these many loopholes in the U.S. legislation been created? As with invisible hand ... [244] They are created specifically to benefit millionaire politicians, corporate interests rather than the voters they are supposed to represent. That is the American political reality—the corporate advantages are created in the legislative process and every act of injustice becomes perfectly legal.

According to *OpenSecrets.org*, The Center for Responsive Politics, an army of lobbyists around Washington, D.C., is actively involved in representing the interests of big businesses to leverage legislation.[245] Lobbyists are well versed in political

---

[244] The famous phrase by Adam Smith in his book, *The Wealth of Nations*, describing the functioning the free market.
[245] Opensecrets.org names 10,600 to 14,800 persons for the years 2007 to 2015. https://www.opensecrets.org/lobby/ [consulted October 14,

party affiliations. For every member of Congress, it is estimated that there are at least 23 lobbyists trying to influence that person's vote to push an agenda of special interests. In other words, 535 senators and representatives, add up to 12,300 lobbyists all pushing for their own cause.[246]

Candidates and members of Congress need funds to finance their campaigns to pay for the very expensive airtime on TV. Lobbying groups supported by specific industries and interest groups support Congressional members with donations, with the intention of covertly influencing legislation. This indirect support enables the election of Representatives, who know the needs of their campaign supporters—and feel a pressing obligation to accommodate them.

It is not the American people influencing Congress; it is the special interests of a few. And their motto? "You scratch my back, I'll scratch yours".

The lobbyists have expressed their needs for their particular industry or concern to Congress members. Those industries' special needs are now "in good hands"; the legislative text will be tweaked and formulated as needed. Laws passed during the legislative session are legitimate, democratically developed and unassailable. By now, you are well aware that legislation has been prepared and bent to suit specific industries, or to support the wealthy. All the while, the American public at large believes that the Representatives have been elected to defend democratic values and represent their interests—and the American people believe that this will indeed happen.

I state that this could not be further from the truth. American politics are influenced and impacted by lobbying activities—on

2015].
[246] Face The Facts USA, Power in Numbers: Lobbyists Have Congress Covered, January 14, 2013.

issues including taxation, environmental protection, contaminated oil fields, medical benefits, social security, and lack of sufficient pension funds for the elderly, and more. The imbalance of income, wealth, and economic structure is a result of the faulty American legislative process.

Distorted Democratic Principles

We have an economic imbalance today. The super-rich and the large companies have extremely strong political power. They use functions of society and turn them to their own benefit. They do not give back a fair share to society. Democracy calls for balance, primarily by strengthening the weaker members and taming the economically stronger ones.

The nations of the so-called Western World—namely the U.S., Canada, Western Europe, Australia, and New Zealand—have a model of democracy in coexistence with market economy. They are functioning well and lead the world economy. I define "economy" as the supply of goods and services to society, and "democracy" as a form of government in which the people elect political leaders and representatives. Both the elected and the voters have an equally important role in ensuring the balance and health of democracy; tension is to be expected because of conflicting interests. An ideal democracy is a power play of interests where the outcome still manages to be as fair as possible to as many players as possible.

In an economic sense, the rules of a capitalistic market economy support the big players, the clever entrepreneur, and the fair and honest manufacturer. When a business is successful, with many clients and a high level of production, it tends to grow. Economies of scale, the price mechanism, and the correct combination of workforce and materials all help to guarantee the business's income and wealth. An economy of scale— proportionate savings costs gained by higher production levels, i.e., that a higher volume of production yields lower unit costs and boosts sales—provides room and resources for research, development, and improvements, which lead in turn to further improvements and savings. Companies following these strategies remain successful in the market, as the market economy is driven to produce more at lower costs in order to capture the market potential. The economy functions well when products and services are manufactured and offered according to the principles of demand and supply.

In short, entering the market is an encounter with society. In the course of bringing goods and services to the market, producers must take into account what impact their product has on society (e.g., paint containing lead would needed to be eliminated from the market and replaced with another product because of health hazards). Individual producers have to meet society's needs, as they have to get the necessary government approvals to manufacture and market their products or services. It is not easy, however, to produce the best product at the right time, at high quality and in the right quantity to meet demand *and* to make a profit. A successful business owner provides timely delivery, high quality, and fair pricing.

Democracy is the political arm of the market economy in the capitalistic world, and it regulates the economy with legislation. The regulation of society is nothing new. The Code of Hammurabi, the oldest codification of society rules, was created 3,700 years ago; its 282 laws regulated the everyday life of the Mesopotamian people.[247] In today's democratic society, laws are created, not only for trade and taxes, but also for education, health, security, environment, foreign policy, defense, and more.

Legislation sets the rules for fair pay, guarantees the fulfillment of contractual agreements and other obligations, protects the individual and the environment (e.g., by banning lead from paint supplies), and helps prepare for future infrastructure planning. Regulations limit economic activities for some people and unlock possibilities for others. Democracy, in this sense, offers the basic rules for living in society; it is a social construct to re-balance influence and power.

The coexistence of regulating (e.g., manufacturing goods) and providing (e.g., goods and services) improves everyone's quality of life. It protects the rich and the poor, as well as large and small businesses. In the western world, the interaction between democracy and the market economy has been very successful for a long time. For a majority of people, it has offered a decent life, including food, housing, health, and culture. The laws of democracy apply to all. That is its recipe for success.

The Distortion

Are our politicians representing or fighting for the good of the average American citizen? The democratic principle has been warped. The political system allows the economic elite and big corporations to influence legislation such that economic rules are strengthened in their favor. Many laws no longer limit these entities' activities, but, instead, reinforce their advantages. The tax burdens of the super-rich have dropped disproportionately

---

[247] Hammurabi, the 6th Babylonian King, ruled from 1792 to 1750 BC. The Code was discovered in 1901 by archeologists in today's Persia. Wikipedia, "Code of Hammurabi" [consulted April 14, 2015].

due to legal loopholes in the tax laws. Other laws allow Corporate America to evade, avoid, and circumvent taxes in grand style. The democratic goal of balancing income differences is rarely effective; as a result, Congressional preferential treatment of the rich and large corporations has eroded the spirit of democracy.

Many rich Americans and corporations are against most regulations, which they view as "limiting their freedom." They would prefer that all legislation lead to their benefit and personal gain. Therefore, the dominance of economic rules in their favor makes for an undemocratic society, and the coexistence of economy and democracy becomes obsolete.

Democracy has one pitfall: Freedom is guaranteed to everyone. This beautiful characteristic can ironically lead to democracy's very demise. Mike Lofgren, author and former Republican congressional aide, wrote in an article for *Truthout*: "As [German-American political theorist] Hannah Arendt observed, a disciplined minority of totalitarians using the instruments of a democratic government can undermine democracy itself."[248]

For some people, "freedom" means enjoying the power to manipulate the system and create opportunities in their favor, as a way to achieve success for themselves. The result is an unbalanced society that is eroding the democratic system. There are clear signs that the United States is exposed to this danger today.

---

[248] Mike Lofgren, "Goodbye to All That: Reflection of a GOP Operative Who Left the Cult," *Truthout*, http://www.truth-out.org/goodbye-all-reflections-gop-operative-who-left-cult/1314907779, and quoted in Mann/Ornstein, *ante*, p. 55.

Form and Content of a Political Mandate

The United States is the founder of modern democracy and the oldest existing democratic polity in the world. The U.S. Constitution and the Bill of Rights are landmarks and milestones in the history of humanity. The United States is a republic with limited office terms, in contrast to a Monarchy. Congress and the government work as a democracy with rules like "one man, one vote", decision making by majorities, and the right of free expression. As the legislators vote on legislations exclusively, the U.S. is a representative democracy.

Citizens have been experiencing the gaps between theory and reality—the bleak space between lofty, idealistic ideas and everyday tangible struggles—since the country's birth as an independent nation. Some of the founding fathers of the new nation, for example, promoted the equality of men—yet they themselves were slave owners. Slavery was legally abolished in 1864; however, more than 100 years passed before African-American citizens were recognized as equal. Reality rarely reflects ideals.

Once westward expansion began, in the 1800s, Native Americans, who have lived throughout North America for centuries, lost their innate rights to the land and to the preservation of their nationalities. They became targets of genocide. The Federal Government refused to recognize the legality and the ownership of the Native Americans' traditional homelands and sent settlers West with the promise of "free land" and the hope of a "new life", completely forsaking some human lives for the sake of other humans' comfort. America has actually not been a defender nor promoter of democracy at home or around the world.

It is no secret that American military interventions worldwide have, for the most part, been driven by pure self-interest. During the 1954 U.S.-backed military coup in Guatemala, democratically-elected President Arbenz and his government were replaced by a dictatorship; this move was made, much like a sliding pawn on a global checkerboard, in order to defend tax privileges of the United Fruit Company which was based in Boston. Guatemala's legacy from this undemocratic dominance was a horrific forty-year-long civil war.

The United Fruit Company prospered, though.

When party politicians bask in the results of their electoral victories ("We have the agenda") or when formal voting restrictions are sought to the detriment of the other party (voting only with a mandatory photo ID is "going to kick Democrats in the butt"), Americans show a lop-sided understanding of democracy focused on form. Something is missing. That something is *content.*

The *form*, or legislative process, of democracy is distinct from the *content* of democracy. The "form" stands for the formal, procedural half of democracy. Correct ballot procedures, correct counting, correct identification of citizens for voting—these must be fulfilled to achieve a democratically-elected Congress, i.e. a democratic process. The "content" of democracy, however, is designed to ensure that the legislation produces a democratic outcome. A Republican-dominated Congress, for example, is elected to act, vote, and execute in order to satisfy democracy as a political form of government on behalf of all citizens. For the democratic process to operate as it is intended to, lawmakers must be elected democratically, and the legislation they pass must lead to democratic results. Democratic form/process and content/result are indispensably connected and interdependent.

The American ideology focuses on political party outcome rather than democratic outcome. Election or voting results are considered democratic when goals and objectives have been met and the party's goals and mission have been satisfied. This understanding is too narrow and insufficient. The defeat in an election, or of a substantive issue, means a loss of prestige, power, and influence. The loser waits for the next opportunity and hopes for the next win. Every effort is made to push through the majority party's agenda; the other party's values are ignored or rejected. In an atmosphere of victory and defeat, there is no room for compromise. Competition tramples cooperation. Party politics have turned into a battlefield; currently, Washington politics are at a stalemate.

When a deputy is elected democratically, his or her commitment to form legislation in favor of democratic content is subjective to his or her personal agenda and interests. He or she may support laws that are undemocratic, or that favor his or her party or special interest groups. State legislators also have the Constitutional responsibility to determine the boundaries of their districts; we have analyzed in prior sections of this book that such power typically leads to gerrymandering and tampered outcomes. The result can be an uneven representation of voters and the dysfunctional allocation of elected seats. Although this manipulation of votes is legal, it too often leads to undemocratic consequences.

When voting on specific tax laws, legislators have further opportunity to create undemocratic outcomes. Tax loopholes are one exemplary result, as they serve a very specific group of people or industries. The same scenario happens with voting restrictions. A lawfully elected legislator may decide to pass a law preventing some citizens from exercising their rights to vote, which is, in essence, undemocratic. The American electorate is not sensitive enough to these actions that depreciate and diminish their government.

Democracy is the acceptance of basic principles for all. The victories of the opposing party must be accepted and respected. Political life in a democracy includes other opinions and compromise. It is about working together to achieve a basic underlying and all-encompassing goal: the preservation of our nation and the wellbeing of its citizens. That's how it *should* be, anyway.

On the contrary, the United States is currently on its way to a Libertarian social order. Government distrust is widespread. Even the introduction of mandatory health insurance has been perceived as hostile government interference in the private sector. According to the 2010 Patient Protection and Affordable Care Act, a specific framework was supposed to be implemented by private insurance companies, which cater to the American idea of giving preference to private entities over state-run entities. Therefore, the law should have been successful.

Because of the American glorification of one kind of individual over all other kinds of individuals, however, the benefits of mandatory health insurance are overlooked. Despite a myriad of examples of illnesses that lead to the loss of homes and the dissolution of pension funds, too many Americans remain unconvinced that nationwide compulsory health insurance makes sense. If you get sick, tough luck. And if you die, you die...

There are clear signs of a plutocracy in Washington.[249] The principle that money rules the world applies worldwide and is easy to prove. It has revealed itself in increments. The

---

[249] Ronald P. Formisano, *Plutocracy in America, How Increasing Inequality Destroys the Mittle Class and Exploits the Poor* (JHU Press, 2015) and other books.

penetration of American politics by economic power-plays and tactics to influence legislation have led to a greatly changed democracy—so much so, say Mann and Ornstein, that even conservative circles are concerned about the impact of their own grassroots and fringe supporters.[250] This concern marks the depth of these changes and ignites questions: Will a new form of democracy emerge to change the country or will the U.S. return to basic values and a familiar course of action?

The proof for a plutocracy is the behavior of rich supporters of political parties. The Koch brothers were infuriated in mid-2017 that their billions of dollars of political donations have not rewritten the tax code or repealed the Affordable Care Act.[251] They live in the conviction that they can buy any political topics that determine the life of the majority of the Americans. In a true democracy, all citizens have an equal voice in their government, regardless of how rich or poor they are.

Will Libertarian values become the standard of American society? If so, how would they influence daily life? Will every road be a toll road? Will we eliminate public schools? Would every step taken on private property be billed?

Seriously, think about it.

Freedom and Protection

Freedom has always been a core American value. For an American entrepreneur, employer, or employee, it also goes hand-in-hand with innovation: the liberty to freely market new

---

[250] Mann/Ornstein, *ante.*
[251] Steve Peoples, "Donors to GOP, No Cash Until Action on Health Care, Taxes", *U.S. News*, June 26, 2017.
https://www.usnews.com/news/politics/articles/2017-06-26/koch-urgency-conservative-network-fears-closing-window

ideas and products. The concept of freedom gives Libertarian Americans the certainty that the individual can succeed or survive alone, without the need for partnership or society. Therefore, as the reasoning goes, taxes are unnecessary; it is not important to organize for a common goal as a group or as a collective.

So that this does *not* happen and so that all people's interests are protected, we need freedom within a specific context. It is my conviction that freedom can be an illusion and a pitfall; freedom as a value in and of itself is not sufficient. To enjoy freedom at its best, we need protection through regulation. The Federal Government is a guarantor of freedom for all and it has the responsibility to protect all of its citizens.

In *The Unwinding: An Inner History of New America*, author George Packer presents a haunting example of failed regulations and the lack of protected freedoms through the story of Tammy Thomas, who worked for 20 years at an auto supply company.[252] A part of her salary was deducted every month to be paid into her company pension fund. She had a vested interest in her retirement. And she slept soundly at night regarding the matter since everything seemed to be right on track.

In 2010, her Ohio neighborhood was hit hard by a wave of job layoffs; the company where she worked also filed for bankruptcy. Tammy, almost 50 at the time, was dismissed and her pension fund was provided to her as a lump sum. She received a cash payment of $140,000. Under U.S. law, about 40% of that cash payment was taxed. She invested the remaining amount with help of a friend. After a few years, however, the money was gone—someone cheated her of the money.

---

[252] George Packer, *The Unwinding: An Inner History of the New America* (New York: Farrar, Strauss and Giroux, 2013), p. 37.

Why was her pension fund paid out to her before she reached retirement age? In a good model of a retirement system, the funds should be placed into a blocked retirement account until retirement. Social legislation must ensure the protection of pensions, regardless of whether a company goes out of business or dismisses an employee. When a worker moves from one job to another, the pension funds must follow, untouched. Later, when the retiree has access to the pension fund, (e.g., in the form of an annuity), the funds received can then be taxed as annual income. Taxation before retirement reduces the amount in the fund at the wrong time and makes it difficult for the account to grow. Premature disbursement of pension funds is a poverty trap. Tammy Thomas followed U.S. law and lost everything.

It could happen to anybody. Americans are not well-versed in planning far ahead financially for themselves. For that reason, social legislation is needed and must be strictly applied. A 25-year old typically does not think about retirement or a pension fund. However, years of saving can increase pension assets. Having a secure pension fund is essential, and it must be protected by federal regulations to prevent younger people from accessing these funds before they retire.

The Failure of Democracy

The aggressive, non-compromising atmosphere within Congress since the 1980s has politically polarized the United States. The Republican Party, with its Libertarian principles and desire to enforce its agenda by any means possible, is the main reason for this deadlock. The Democratic Party had to follow the new rules and copied the behavior. The outright rejection of President Obama's ideas, for example, simply because they were his ideas, became the *modus operandi* between 2008 and 2016. A trend has ensued where special interests dominate, subjugate, and overpower Congress. The dysfunctional situation extends from candidate selection to party loyalty and beyond.

Princeton University researchers Gilens and Page stated, in 2014, that the American political system has slowly transformed from a democracy to an oligarchy, where the wealthy elites hold control and exercise the most power.[253] The two researchers collected data from 1,800 laws at the State and Federal levels from 1981 to 2002. They compared the results of political changes in legislation with public opinion on the original issues. The results nearly always reflected the interests of those who hold 10% of the nation's wealth, as well as lobbyists and the business community, but rarely the interests of average Americans. For example, 83-91% of Americans advocated for background checks prior to weapons purchases, but, due to the influence of the National Rifle Association and other pro-gun lobbyists, Congress remains mute on the issue. Likewise, Congress often ignores global warming and related environmental issues, even as the concern about preserving and protecting Mother Nature is widespread.

Religious Values and Politics

The first European immigrants felt connected to their religious values upon their arrival in the New World. They fled their homelands to live in accordance with their faith, respecting the Christian way of humanity and charity. Although America is a country that segregates religion from government, elements of

---

[253] Brendan James, Princeton Study: "U.S. No Longer An Actual Democracy," *TPM Talking Points Memo*, April 18, 2014.

faith have been woven into the fabric of the nation. As quoted from *The Robert Bellah Reader*: "Considering the separation of church and state, how is a president justified in using the word 'God' at all? The answer is that the separation of church and state has not denied the political realm a religious dimension."[254]

Even today, the average American is attached to some sort of religious community. Churches and religious meetings are well-attended across the nation. The virtues of charity and humility are praised and valued. At some family dinner tables, prayers are expressed in gratitude to God and good neighbors. Many Americans continue to be religiously fervent and try to live with good intentions toward the rest of humanity.

Politicians also invoke the protective hand of God, whether they believe in God or not. Presidents end every speech with: "God bless the American people and God bless America." Coins and bills are imprinted with "In God We Trust." Children are taught from an early age to recite the Pledge of Allegiance, which includes the phrase "one nation under God." Politicians also refer to the nation as the "Republic of Virtue."[255]

The reference to religious values is an expression of ethical principles. Political reality, however, is not driven by these virtues. Using religion in politics actually infringes on religious freedom. The separation of Church and State is a founding principle of the United States. Nonetheless, religious values continue to influence politics, but they are not used in their ethical context: there are no efforts to get to the root of the urgent problems in America, such as chronic poverty, for example.

---

[254] *The Robert Bellah Reader*, Edited by Robert N. Bellah and Steven M. Tipton, Duke University Press, 2006, p.228.

[255] Daniel N. Robinson, *American Ideals: Founding a "Republic of Virtue"* (Video, Chantilly, VA: The Great Courses, The Teaching Company, 2004).

Core values are conveniently forgotten by politicians who have Libertarian goals. The Tea Party movement, for instance, is fundamentally religious and yet neglects religious values when it acts politically. If you listen to politicians talk about health insurance or immigration, there is little talk of charity or support for fellow humans. What has happened to American values?

History Teaches the Community

Individual success is the core of American ideology. This nation lives by the example of fearless explorers, such as Lewis and Clark, who explored a path from St. Louis to the Pacific Ocean.[256] Their trip to and from their destination in unknown territory— up the Missouri River, over the Continental Divide in the Rocky Mountains—lasted three years from 1804 to 1806. Others who pioneered to the West also deserve the attributes of *explorer* and *lone warrior*. Their sojourns made the road safe for homesteaders; their courage made the journey "off the beaten path" possible. After many decades, the journey toward individual happiness and the pursuit of purpose and pioneering has shifted to a different frontier: the economic battle of life.

The naïve immigrant and the courageous, westward-bound explorer are characters eternally reflected in the American soul. They still embody what it means to be "American" for many of today's Americans. The driving force has always been the fight for survival, the idea of attaining a better life, and the pursuit of personal happiness. All of that was, and is, associated with wealth and prosperity. Many things had to be mastered by individual efforts. Many times, on such journeys, the only person

---

[256] Ken Burns, *Lewis & Clark, The Journey of the Corps of Discovery* (Washington DC: Public Broadcast Service [PBS], 1997).

who could save you was yourself. The crossing of a desert or the successful defense against bandits and outlaws, however, frequently ended with the arrival in a town: the conclusion of a community's embrace and welcome.

This, too, is an element of the American legend. A settlement with food, hot water, beds, and trustworthy people is always found included in the stories of classic western movies. Even non-fiction accounts include—at least for the survivors—their eventual arrival in a town where there are services and products available that only can be made in a community of men. A good example of this is the family history of the famous piano-making company Steinway & Sons, which began in 1797 with the birth of company founder Heinrich Engelhard Steinweg, who would migrate from Germany to New York to make his piano-constructing dream a reality. Their story parallels those of many immigrants who sought shelter with fellow countrymen or family members, and started their new lives in such communities.[257] It is an illusion to believe that a full life can be achieved solely through individual effort and without any interpersonal interactions. The individual is responsible for himself in many contexts, yes. Remember, however, most human beings are members of several communities—and this exactly as we desire it. The communities of family, of kindred spirits, and of neighbors have the potential to create the ideal environment of every human being.

The hard times and individual struggles are only part of the picture, but they are what society remembers. They are glorified and they reign in the memory of the American soul and dream. It

---

[257] Richard K. Liebermann, *Steinway & Sons* (New Haven and London: Yale University Press, 1995).

is easy to forget the context in which these success stories are
written (and by which they were, in great part, made possible).

Part 6:
Restore Trust

The Essance of Democracy

What is Democracy?

Fundamentally, democracy is a political form of civil coexistence. Its rules and principles allow people of different opinions to live together and share ideas. French diplomat and political scientist Alexis de Tocqueville, as quoted in Professor William R. Cook's book *Tocqueville and the American Experiment*, long ago defined the concept as thus:

> "The essence of democracy is equality. Democracy depends on broad participation of citizens in public life at the local level. Equality leads people to withdraw into themselves. The success of democracy hinges on vibrant local political and social institutions that will limit the centralization of administrative power and encourage people to be active in politics."[258]

I agree with this explanation wholeheartedly. I believe that democracy, in a substantive sense, means the recognition and acceptance of different values. The discovery process in a

---

[258] William R. Cook, *Tocqueville and the American Experiment* (Chantilly, VA: The Great Courses, The Teaching Company, 2004), Video/booklet p. 6.

democracy must be able to call upon common values to fulfill political coexistence. We live in a world with many different cultures, speaking many different languages, offering a variety of talents and gifts, containing different religious beliefs, and with each of us wanting to fulfill our desires, values, and needs. Democracy can integrate existing societal differences and enable the wellbeing and dignity of all citizens.

To achieve a healthy society, everyone must comply with rules and regulations. It begins with a partnership and family, forming the first stage of coexistence. This transcends to the bigger "family" circle of the tribe: the village or city, followed by the county, the state, and the nation. Ideally, we end up as citizens of the world - each of us co-existing as fellow human beings. Our nations become formal societies based on the desire, and the need, to enforce equality and justice.

The democratic government of a country must also have principles and enforce laws that govern behavior and incorporate the opinions and concerns of its citizens. The population must also accept a democratic social order. Democracy knows that there are rules with the ability to limit one person and protect another; democracy seeks, instead, to ensure that no one can claim more rights than anyone else. Everyone is equal. The weak are protected against the strong, and all have the same political rights. Some laws, however, such as those governing income tax, must compensate for differences. Citizens with a higher income pay more taxes as compared to those who have a lower income. That is the notion of fairness.

Protecting American democracy has little to do with weapons. It has less to do with the infiltration of other societies and the threat of external governments than it does with the unity or fracture within our own nation's borders. That is because democracy is, at its core, a state of mind that recognizes democratic values which benefit both the individual and society.

A New Perspective of Government

Across the political spectrum, Americans blame and criticize the Federal Government for high tax rates and overspending. They know that 50% of taxes generated each year are spent on social programs, including Social Security, Medicaid, and food stamps, among hundreds of other programs. The general consensus across much of America seems to be that those who receive social benefits are lazy, entitled, and manipulative. Here is the missing piece of the puzzle, however: Corporate America, with its focus on the bottom line, has created a society of helpless wage earners who end up in the vicious cycle of social programs.

"Governments play a number of roles in an economy. For example, they create the legal environment in which an economy functions, engage in activities to promote domestic trade and industry, impose regulations, and engage in production."

Donald J. Harreld, PhD
"An Economic History of the World since 1400"
The Great Courses, 2016

Americans need to understand that the lifeblood of a corporation is not the same as their very own. The human life-force may be food, water, and shelter; the life-force of a corporation is its human resources. Yet the driving force and motivation of a corporation is the pursuit of profit, and its leaders are willing to do anything to preserve that. To attain this monetary goal, corporations fight for the right to pay low wages, ignore sensitive environmental issues, and do not care about infrastructure or long-term communal consequences of their actions.

The reality is individuals and small business taxpayers are the ones subsidizing the profits of Corporate America. Corporations are the biggest welfare babies out there; the American people pay to suckle them with their tax bills. And ironically, the whole time, these same Americans are being fed the notion that the real problem is embodied by the "lazy, poor, and downtrodden". They underestimate the impact of a low minimum wage on the Federal budget and the U.S. economy. Simply put, corporations have passed off their social responsibilities to the government. This is the pivotal issue that Americans across the political spectrum have been conditioned not to understand.

Conclusive Call to Action

Considering the various facts outlined throughout this book, it should come as no surprise that my belief is that the state of American democracy is in very poor shape. There is a widespread feeling of malaise in the country, and changes are required to reduce the discomfort. So what is next for America?

Ineffective politics can be revamped only when there is a political will to change. To begin with, it is important to find common ground and a strong intention to create change. The advantages of democracy are not offered freely; citizen action is necessary, such as supporting equal voting rights, becoming active in the political system, and reminding legislators of their campaign promises.

Here are some suggestions—simple, basic, yet with the potential to wake society up and help make a difference—for change. Remember that sometimes, a little bit goes a long way. And any journey always begins with *a single step.* It's up to you to take it.

Strengthen Democracy

- Feel first as an American citizen, and then as a party member.
- Be or become active in your local party. Restore the concept of "government by the people, for the people." A democratic republic calls for the elected authority to mandate the will of the people. That's what we, as Americans, need to strive for and demand of our government.
- Take part in all primaries, caucus and elections on State and Federal Level.
- Make an effort to set up independent electoral commissions in each state to abolish gerrymandering and other voter restrictions; the concerns and perspectives of the people must be represented equally in Congress. Gerrymandering is fraudulent and must be abolished.
- Voting restrictions do not uphold the spirit of democracy-on the contrary! The fundamental requirement of good representation is still "one person, one vote."
- Vote to support your values, not your dream. American voters must be more vigilant when electing officials. Learn to define your own needs, wants, and concerns and then vote for the candidates who will support those same

needs and concerns. Trustworthy candidates are essential.

- Remember: The American Declaration of Independence designed the vision of America as a nation defined by its commitment to the idea of equality.
- Be in favor of regulating campaign financing; big money must not influence the outcome of an election. Currently, members of Congress are being heavily influenced by big-money lobbyists. The promises made during campaigns must be kept by those elected.
- Support repealing the Citizens United vs. Federal Election Commission decision. This Supreme Court ruling classifies corporations as people and places no limits to campaign financing.
- Be in favor of tax paying to local, state and federal authorities. This will fund better infrastructure, good public schools, high security, and more.

Fight Poverty

- Attention must be paid to poverty traps.
- Be and feel responsible for all Americans. Your individual destiny is related to bigger units: family, county, state, and nation.
- Support making pension funds mandatory.
- Support including part-time employees in social legislation to avoid employment poverty traps.
- Be in favor a higher minimum wage.
- Stop subsidizing corporations indirectly; low minimum wage increases the cost of welfare.
- Favor the removal of the cap of taxable earnings from Social Security contributions.

- Support maintaining mandatory health insurance. Adjust the Affordable Health Care Act to make it successful for everyone or help promoting Medicare for all.
- Be ready and willing to make monthly contributions toward retirement and healthcare to prevent poverty.
- Solidarity is necessary; young people must buy health insurance.
- Poverty of the nation's senior citizens must be addressed.

Reform the Economy

- Track the performance of the new Republican tax law (2017). Check its effects on the middle class and the poor. Some current U.S. tax laws support preferential treatment of large companies and the super-rich. The idea that the powerful and rich should pay their fair share (i.e., a larger share toward the cost of government spending) should be the mainstream American position.
- Pension plan assets must be outsourced to an independent entity; a pension plan fund must not appear on the employer's balance sheet.
- Eliminating poverty is the only way to reduce welfare spending and, ultimately, a big part of the Federal budget deficit.

The United States was once known for its rigorous anti-trust laws and their strict application in the beginning of the 20th century. Rules against monopolies, cartels, market power, and insider trading helped U.S. democracy and the market economy to survive and expand. These rules are very powerful, regulating the country's economic development and defending the spirit of free market economy. Strong regulations for banking, health insurance mergers, and media concentration are still a must. New restrictions are necessary.[259]

In the minds of most Americans, democracy is limited to the formal process of elections and the activities of majority-building for legislation. This, in and of itself, is extremely incomplete. The full functioning of democracy is the interaction of form and content. One basic task of democracy is to guarantee social equality and the respect of the individual within a community. Democracy is a principle intended to protect all, including the less fortunate. The effort to create a balance between rich and poor, between young and old, between strong and weak, and between big and small must take precedence. Changes in favor of a democratic attitude are to be found mainly in the cultivation of an ideology, which is responsible for how laws are framed. Laws must support equality. Laws must support the people. Laws must bring justice.

Let us get started!

---

[259] Dave Danforth, "Monopoly law is a needed artifact," *Aspen Daily News,* April 3, 2016.

Amongst the novel objects that attracted my attention during my stay in the United States, nothing struck me more forcibly than the general equality of condition among the people. I readily discovered the prodigious influence which this primary fact exercises on the whole course of society; it gives a peculiar direction to public opinion, and a peculiar tenor to the laws; it imparts new maxims to the governing authorities, and peculiar habits to the governed.

I soon perceived that the influence of this fact extends far beyond the political character and the laws of the country, and that it has no less empire over civil society than over the government; it creates opinions, gives birth to new sentiments, founds novel customs, and modifies whatever it does not produce. The more I advanced in the study of American society, the more I perceived that this equality of condition is the fundamental fact from which all others seem to be derived, and the central point at which all my observations constantly terminated.

-Alexis de Tocqueville, *Democracy in America*

Bibliography

Books

The Robert Bellah Reader, Edited by Robert N. Bellah and Steven M. Tipton, Duke University Press, 2006.

Ari **Berman**, *Give Us the Ballot: The Modern Struggle for Voting Rights in America* (New York: Farrar, Straus and Giroux, 2015).

Ronald P. **Formisano**, *Plutocracy in America, How Increasing Inequality Destroys the Mittle Class and Exploits the Poor* (JHU Press, 2015).

Erich **Fromm**, *To Have or To Be?* (New York: Harper & Row, 1976).

Robert M. **Gates**, *Duty: Memoirs of a Secretary of War* (New York: Borzoi Book/Alfred Knopf Publishing, 2014).

Thom **Hartman**, *Screwed: The Undeclared War Against the Middle Class* (San Francisco: Berrett-Koehler Publishers, Inc., 2006).

Robert G. **Kaiser**, *So Much Damn Money: The Triumph of Lobbying and the Corrosion of American Government* (New York: Vintage Books, 2009).

Richard K. **Liebermann**, *Steinway & Sons* (New Haven and London: Yale University Press, 1995).

Thomas E. **Mann** and Norman J. **Ornstein**, *It's Even Worse Than it Looks: How the American Constitutional System Collided with the New Politics of Extremism* (New York: Basic Books, 2012).

George **Packer**, *The Unwinding: An Inner History of the New America* (New York: Farrar, Straus and Giroux, 2013).

Ayn **Rand**, *The Virtue of Selfishness* (New York: New American Library, 1964).

Ayn **Rand**, *The Fountainhead* (Indianapolis: Bobbs-Merrill Company, 1943)

Ayn **Rand**, *Atlas Shrugged* (New York: Random House, 1957)

Roberto **Saviano**, *Gomorrah: A Personal Journey into the Violent International Empire of Naples' Organized Crime System* (New York: Picador/Farrar, Straus and Giroux, 2008).

Gregory L. **Schneider**, *The Conservative Century: From Reaction to Revolution* (New York: Rowman and Littlefield Publishers Inc., 2009).

Magazines – Newspapers – Reviews

Edward **Abbey**, "Down the River with Henry Thoreau," Manuscript Entry of November 9, 1980.

Doug **Altner**, "Why Do 1.4 Million Americans Work At Walmart, With Many More Trying To?", *Forbes,* November 27, 2013.

Beat **Ammann**, "Der Weltmeister im Inhaftieren geht über die Bücher" (The world-champion is re-examining the situation), *Neue Zürcher Zeitung,* October 7, 2015.

Americans for Tax Reform, http://www.atr.org/

Charles **Babington** and Laurie **Kellermann**, "In Congress, income inequality comes with breakfast, lunch," *Aspen Daily News* (Associated Press), May 4, 2015.

Nicholas **Bakalar**, "Nearly 20 Million Have Gained Health Insurance Since 2010", *The New York Times,* May 22, 2017

Thomas **Barrabi**, "Tax reform windfall: These companies are hiking pay, delivering bonuses", *FOXBusiness,* March 7, 2018

Chris **Barth**, "29 Companies That Paid Millions For Lobbying (And Didn't Pay Taxes)", *Forbes Magazine,* December 14, 2011

Steven **Brill**, "Bitter Pill, Why Medical Bills Are Killing Us," Special report, *Time Magazine*, March 4, 2013.

Arthur C. **Brooks**, "The Conservative Heart" (brochure), *The American Enterprise Institute*, 2015.

Ronald **Brownstein**, "The Four Quadrants of Congress," *National Journal,* January 30, 2011.

Paul **Buchheit**, "How American Corporations and the Super Rich Steal From the Rest of Us," *AlterNet,* December 28, 2014.

Philip **Bump**, "Mitch McConnell says improved economy is result of 'the expectation of a new Republican Congress.' Um, probably not," *The Washington Post,* January 7, 2015.

Opensecrets.org, **Center for Responsive Politics**. Lobbying, top industries, consulted on June 26, 2017, https://www.opensecrets.org/lobby/top.php?indexType=i

Center on Budget and Policy Priorities (CBPP): "Policy Basics: Where Do Our Tax Dollars Go?" October 04, 2017. http://www.cbpp.org/research/policy-basics-where-do-our-federal-tax-dollars-go

Russ **Choma**, "Millionaires' Club: For First Time, Most Lawmakers are Worth $1 Million-Plus," *OpenSecrets.org*, January 9, 2014.

Noam **Chomsky**, "How America's Great University System is Being Destroyed. Faculty are increasingly hired on the Walmart model as temps," *AlterNet,* February 28, 2014. Refers to *The Federal Reserve Board protocol*, "Testimony of Chairman Alan Greenspan," February 26, 1997.

Noam **Chomsky**, "Why People know so much about Sports But so Little about World Affairs," *AlterNet,* September 15, 2014.

Greta **Christina**, "7 Things People Who Say They're 'Fiscally Conservative But Socially Liberal' Don't Understand," *AlterNet,* May 20, 2015.

"**Citizens United v. Federal Election Commission**," *Ballotpedia,* https://ballotpedia.org/Citizens_United_v._Federal_Election_Com mission

Michael **Cohen**, "How for-profit prisons have become the biggest lobby no one is talking about," *The Washington Post,* April 28, 2015.

Constitution of the United States, Article I, Section 4.

Consumer Reports, "Why is health care so expensive? Why it's so high, how it affects your wallet—and yes, what you can do about it," September 2014 https://www.consumerreports.org/cro/magazine/2014/11/it-is-time-to-get-mad-about-the-outrageous-cost-of-health-care/index.htm

Leslie **Cuadra**, "List of World's Largest Creditor and Debtor Nations,"
Financial Sense, August 31, 2011.
http://www.financialsense.com/contributors/leslie-
cuadra/2011/08/31/list-of-worlds-largest-creditor-and-debtor-
nations, consulted May 20, 2015.

Juliette **Cubanski**, Giselle **Casillas** and Anthony **Damico**, "Poverty
Among Seniors: An Updated Analysis of National and State Level
Poverty Rates Under the Official and Supplemental Poverty
Measures," *The Henry J. Kaiser Family Foundation*, June 10, 2015

Juliette **Cubanski** and Tricia **Neumann**, "The Facts on Medicare
Spending and Financing", *The Henry J. Kaiser Family Foundation*,
July 18, 2017

Tara **Culp-Ressler**, "The U.S. Has The Most Expensive And Least
Effective Health Care In The Developed World," *ThinkProgress,*
June 16, 2014

Corey **Dade**, "Why New Photo ID Laws Mean Some Won't Vote",
January 28, 2012, NPR,
http://www.npr.org/2012/01/28/146006217/why-new-photo-
id-laws-mean-some-wont-vote.

Dave **Danforth**, "Monopoly law is a needed artifact," *Aspen Daily News,*
April 3, 2016.

Paul **Davidson**, "The job juggle is real. Many Americans are balancing
two, even three gigs," *USA Today*, October 17, 2016.

Tad **deHaven**, "Privatizing Amtrak," Cato Institute: Downsizing the
Federal Government, June 2010.

Jason **DeRusha**, "Good Question: How Many Of Us Still Get A Pension?"
CBS local Minnesota, October 17, 2012.

Jim **Dexter**, "CNN Fact Check: The last president to balance the
budget," *CNN,* February 3, 2010.

Report by the **Democratic members of the U.S. House Committee
on Education and Workforce,** "The Low-Wage Drag on Our
Economy, Wal-Marts low wages and their effect on taxpayers and
economic growth," consulted May 23, 2015.

http://democrats.edworkforce.house.gov/
  sites/democrats.edworkforce.house.gov/files/documents/WalMar
  tReport-.pdf

Kevin **Drum** and Jaeah **Lee**, "3 Charts Why Democrats Went Nuclear on the Filibuster," *Mother Jones,* November 22, 2013.

Patrick **Duggan**, "Why Small Businesses are the Backbone of America," *Pacific Community Ventures*, July 15, 2015, www.pacificcommunityventures.org/2015/07/15/why-small-businesses-are-the-backbone-of-america/

Charles **Duhigg** and Keith **Bradsher**, "How the U.S. Lost Out on iPhone Work," *The New York Times,* January 21, 2012.

Tyler **Durden**, "Broke Kansas To Tax Poor People By Placing $25 Limit on ATM Withdrawals," *Zero Hedge,* May 25, 2015.

David **Espo** and Andrew **Taylor**, "House, Senate panels adopt tough balanced-budget plans," *Aspen Daily News,* March 20, 2015.

Face The Facts USA, Power in Numbers: Lobbyists Have Congress Covered, January 14, 2013.

Peter **Ferrara**, "'Welfare State' Doesn't Adequately Describe How Much America's Poor Control Your Wallet," *Forbes,* June 23, 2013.

FindLaw, "Part Time, Temporary, and Seasonal Employees," 2013.

Elizabeth **Flock**, "5 Things the Government Spends More on Than PBS," *U.S. News and World Report,* October 4, 2012.

Mark **Frauenfelder**, "Dunkin' CEO makes $10 million a year but $15 Dollar minimum wage is 'absolutely outrageous,'" *Boing Boing,* July 26, 2015.

Jessica **Glenza**, "Dismantling Obamacare: what has Trump done and who will it affect?", *The Guardian,* October 13, 2017.

Jeff **Graham**, "Target Hikes Base Wage To $12 An Hour, One-Upping Walmart Despite Earnings Squeeze", *Investor's Business Daily,* March 6, 2018, https://www.investors.com/news/economy/target-hikes-base-wage-to-12-an-hour-above-walmart/

Jon **Greenberg**, "Sanders: One out of four Corporations pay no taxes", *PolitiFact,* September 26, 2013.

Jeff **Griffin**, "The History of Healthcare in America", *JP Griffin Group*, March 7, 2017.

Ryan **Grimm** and Sabrina **Siddiqui**, "Call Time for Congress Shows how Fundraising Dominates Bleak Work Life," *The Huffington Post*, January 8, 2013.

Richard L. **Hasen**, "How Justice Kennedy paved the way for 'Super-PACS' and the return of soft money," *Slate*, October 25, 2011.

Dave **Hogg**, "The Military Paid Pro Sports Teams 10.4 Million For Patriotic Displays, Troop tributes," *SBNation*, November 4, 2015 (The McCain/Flake Report)

Gwen **Ifill** with Michael Dimock, "Pew study finds more polarized Americans increasingly resistant to political compromise," *Rocky Mountain PBS: The Newshour*, June 12, 2014.

Christopher **Ingraham**, "America's most gerrymandered districts", *The Washington Post*, May 15, 2014.

Christopher **Ingraham**, "This is the best explanation of gerrymandering you will ever see. How to steal an election: a visual guide," *The Washington Post*, March 1, 2015.

Ken **Jacobs**, Ian **Perry** and Jenifer **MacGillvary**, "The High Public Cost of Low Wages," *UC Berkeley Labor Center*, April 13, 2015

Brendan **James**, "Princeton Study: U.S. No Longer An Actual Democracy," *TPM (Talking Point Memory)*, April 18, 2014.

Randy **James**, "Food Stamps," *Time Magazine*, September 14, 2009.

KHN **Kaiser Health News**, "Nixon's Plan For Health Reform, His Own Words," September 03, 2009.

Dara **Kam** and John **Lantigua**, "Former Florida GOP leaders say voter suppression was reason they pushed new election law," *Palm Beach Post*, November 25, 2012.

David **Klepper** and Deepti **Hajela**, "For the first time, a U.S. state may single out one industry for a big wage hike, *Business Insider*, July 22. 2015

David **Kocieniewsky**, "G.E.'s Strategies Let It Avoid Taxes Altogether," *The New York Times*, March 24, 2011.

Allison **Kopicki**, "Support Is Thin for Tea Party, but It Retains Its Muscles," *The New York Times*, June 24, 2014.

Andy **Kroll**, "What the FEC?" *Mother Jones,* April 18, 2011.

Paul **Krugman**, "Increase in longevity have been greater for higher earners," *Peter G. Peterson Foundation,* November 21, 2014.

Paul **Krugman**, "Report on the Economic Well-Being on U.S. Households in 2014," *Board of Governors of the Federal Reserve System,* May 2015.

Paul **Krugman**, "The Insecure American," *The New York Times,* May 29, 2015.

Martin **Lanz**, "Viel Bewegung bei den US-Mindestlöhnen" [Some moves on the issue of U.S. minimal wages], *Neue Zürcher Zeitung,* May 26, 2015.

Martin **Lanz**, "Mit Uncle Sam im Rücken" [With Uncle Sam in your back], *Neue Zürcher Zeitung,* July 24, 2015.

William **Lazonick**, "Profits without Prosperity," *Havard Business Review,* September 2014.

William **Lazonick**, "What Apple should do With its Massive Piles of Money," *Harvard Business Review,* October 20, 2014.

Lisa **Leff** and David **Klepper**, "Higher minimum-wage proposals gain ground," *Aspen Daily News,* July 23, 2015.

Dave **Levinthal**, "Koch foundation proposal to college: Teach our curriculum, get millions," *The Center for Public Integrity,* September 12, 2014.

Les **Leopold**, "The 6 Economic Facts of Life in America That Allow the Rich to Run off with our Wealth," *AlterNet,* December 16, 2014.

Michael **Li**, "Citizen-Led State Gerrymandering Reforms Starts to Show Results," *billmoyers.com,* July 13, 2015. http://billmoyers.com/2015/07/13/citizen-led-state-gerrymandering-reforms-start-to-show-results/

Mike **Lofgren**, "Goodbye to All That: Reflection of a GOP Operative Who Left the Cult," *Truthout,* http://www.truth-out.org/goodbye-all-reflections-gop-operative-who-left-cult/ 1314907779

Tamara **Lytle**, "What is wrong with Washington," *AARP Bulletin,* December 2011, p 16.

Werner **Marti**, "Jeb Bush geht in die Offensive" (Jeb Bush takes the offensive), *Neue Zürcher Zeitung,* August 12, 2015.

Merrill **Matthews**, "What Happened to the $2.6 Trillion Social Security Trust Fund?", *Forbes*, July 13, 2011

Kevin **McCoy**, "Apple CEO defends tax tactics at Senate Hearing," *USA TODAY*, May 26, 2013.

Sean **McElwee**, "The great American rip-off: How big-money corruption fuels racial inequality," *Salon,* December 21, 2014.

Signe-Mary **McKernan**, Caroline **Ratcliffe**, and Stephanie R. **Cellini**, "Transitioning In and Out of Poverty", *The Urban Institute,* September 1, 2009.

Ali **Meyer**, "Record 20% of Households on Food Stamps in 2013," *CNSNews.com,* January 21, 2014.

Rashed **Mian**, "NY Moves toward $15 Minimum Wage for Fast Food Workers," *Long Island Press,* July 23, 2015.

Ian **Millhiser**, "Texas Brags To Court That It Drew District Lines To 'Increase The Republican Party's Electoral Prospects,'" *Think Progress*, August 14, 2013.

Ian **Millheiser**, "The Supreme Court's about To Hear a Case That Could Make Partisan Gerrymandering Even Worse," *Think Progress,* February 27, 2015.

Lori **Montgomery**, Jia Lynn **Yang** and Philip **Rucker**, "Mitt Romney releases tax returns", *The Washington Post,* January 24, 2012.

Rick **Moran**, "Percentage of Americans on welfare hits record levels," *American Thinker,* July 9, 2014.

David **Morris**, "Hey Michelle and Barack: Walmart and Amazon are the Problem, not the Solution," *AlterNet,* May 19, 2015.

Tim **Murphy**, "Amazon, Buffet, JPMorgan join forces on health care", *The Associated Press/The Aspen Times,* January 31, 2018.

National Poverty Center, "Poverty in the United States, Frequently Asked Questions," *University of Michigan,* April 23, 2015. http://www.npc.umich.edu/poverty/#3)

Newsmax: "Apple CEO Tells Senate: 'We Pay All the Taxes We Owe,'" *Bloomberg News*, May 21, 2013.

Joe **Nocera**, "Carl Icahn's Bad Advice," *The New York Times*, October 24, 2014.

Grover **Norquist**, "Thomas Piketty, Chronicler of Inequality," *Time Magazine* (double issue), April 27 and May 5, 2015, p 149.

Brendan **Nyhan**, "Voter Fraud is Rare, but Myth is Withspread," *The New York Times,* June 10, 2014.

Patrick **O'Connor**, "Poll Finds Americans Want Parties to Work Together," *The Wall Street Journal*, November 19, 2014.

Norm **Ornstein**, "The Pernicious Effects of Gerrymandering," *National Journal Daily,* December 4, 2014.

Akin **Oyedele**, "Here is the ridiculous amount of cash U.S. companies are stashing overseas," *Business Insider*, March 17, 2015.

Chantal **Panozzo**, "Living in Switzerland ruined me for America and its lousy work culture," *www.vox.com,* July 21, 2015. http://www.vox.com/2015/7/21/8974435/switzerland-work-life-balance

Lynn **Parramore**, "Lazonick: How Superstar Companies Like Apple Are Killing America's High Tech Future," *The Institute for New Economic Thinking,* December 9, 2014.

Vicky **Pelaez**, "The Prison Industries in the United States: Big Business or a New Form of Slavery," *Global Research,* March 31, 2014.

People For the American Way, "People For The American Way Foundation Applauds FL Supreme Court for Striking Down Gerrymandered Districts," July 9, 2015.

People for the American Way, "Report: In Key Races, Margin of Victory Came Close to 'Margin of Disenfranchisement,'" November 07, 2014.

Steve **Peoples**, "Donors to GOP, No Cash Until Action on Health Care, Taxes", *U.S. News,* June 26, 2017. https://www.usnews.com/news/politics/articles/2017-06-26/koch-urgency-conservative-network-fears-closing-window

Elaine **Pofeldt**, "Shocker: 40% of Workers Now Have 'Contingent' Jobs, Says U.S. Government", *Forbes,* May 25, 2015 and "Freelancers Now Make Up 35% Of U.S. Workforce", *Forbes,* October 6, 2016

Scott **Porch**, "Richard Nixon would be 'drummed out' of GOP today as a liberal: 'He passed as much social welfare legislation as Lyndon Johnson'" *Salon*, April 4, 2016.

Catherine **Rampell**, "The Rise of Part-Time Work," *The New York Times*, March 8, 2013.

Erika **Rawes**, "7 things the middle class can't afford anymore," *USA Today,* October 25, 2014.

Robert **Reich**, "Right Wing lies, on Corporate Tax Rate Reform," *The Left Call,* November 30, 2014.

Robert **Reich**, Note on *Facebook*, March 18, 2015.

Robert **Reich**, Posting in *Facebook*, January 9, 2015.

Robert **Reich**, "Colleges, Churches and Non-Profits Doing the Wealthy's Dirty Work," *AlterNet*, April 7, 2015.

Robert **Reich**, "The Rigging of the American Market," *Huffington Post,* November 1, 2015.

Nicholas **Riccardi**, "Washington infighting breeds new independent United States candidates", *Aspen Daily News/Associated Press,* January 26, 2018.

Charles **Riley**, "Tom Perkins' big idea: the Rich should get more votes," *CNN money*, February 14, 2014.

Tim **Roemer**, "Why do Congressmen spend only half of their time serving us?" *Newsweek*, July 29, 2015.

Franklin **Roosevelt**'s Statement on the National Industrial Recovery Act June 16, 1933, cited in the New York Times, March 7, 2014

Steven **Rosenfeld**, "12 Ways the GOP Would Destroy the Country If They Controlled Washington after 2016," *AlterNet,* May 8, 2015.

Richard **Rubin**, "U.S. Companies Are Stashing $2.1 Trillion Overseas to Avoid Taxes," *BloombergBusiness*, March 4, 2015.

Senator Bernie **Sanders**, "What do the Koch Brothers Want?" Homepage: http://www.sanders.senate.gov/koch-brothers, consulted May 8, 2015.

Margot **Sanger-Katz**, "Why Is U.S. Health Care So Expensive? Some of the Reasons You've Heard Turn Out to Be Myths," *The New York Times/The Upshot*, March 13, 2018; based on a study by *The Journal of the American Medical Association.*

Jason **Sattler**, "6 Other Times Republicans Admitted Voting Restrictions Are Just About Disenfranchising Democrats," *The National Memo*, October 25, 2013.

Cathy **Schoen** et al. "How Health Insurance Design Affects Access To Care And Costs, By Income, In Eleven Countries," *Health Affairs* (Health Aff 10.1377/hlthaff.2010.0862, 2010).

Stacey **Selleck**, "Congress Spends More Time Dialing for Dollars Than on Legislative Work", *US Term Limits*, April 2016

Michael D. **Shear**, "Touring Warship, Trump Pushes Plan to Expand Military," *The New York Times,"* March 2, 2017.

Robert **Sherrill**, "The Most Expensive Health Care System in the World," *The Donella Meadows Archive, Voice of a Global Citizen*, Sustainability Institute, (Hartland, VT: no date).

Jeff **Spross**, "Want to end poverty in America? It's pretty simple," *The Week,* January 21, 2015.

"Poverty in the United States, Frequently Asked Questions," *National Poverty Center,* University of Michigan, April 23, 2015 (http://www.npc.umich.edu/poverty/#3)

Robert M. **Stein** and Greg **Vonnahme**, "Election Day Vote Centers und Voter Turnout," *Midwest Political Science Association*, Chicago, IL, April 22-24, 2006.

Katy **Steinmetz**, "Is the on-demand economy taking workers for a ride?" *Time Magazine,* August 3, 2015.

Felix **Stephan**, "Puppenhausprosa der Kapitalisten" ("Dollhouse prose of Capitalists"), *Die Zeit (ZEITonline),* August 17, 2012.

The Commonwealth Fund, "Mirror, Mirror on the Wall: An International Update on the Comparative Performance of American Health Care," *The Commonwealth Fund*, May 15, 2007 and updates to June 16, 2014.

The Pew Center on the States, "Upgrading Democracy: Improving America's Elections by Modernizing States' Voter Registration Systems," November 2010.

U.S. Bureau of Labor Statistics, "The Employment Situation, March 2015," *BLS News Release,* April 3, 2015.

U.S. Catholic Bishops, Poverty USA, an initiative, April 23, 2015. (www.povertyusa.org) http://www.povertyusa.org/the-state-of-poverty/poverty-map-state/#

U.S. Census Bureau. Average income for 2013 is $51,939, 8% less than in 2007. Published on http://en.wikipedia.org/wiki/Household_income_in_the_United_St ates

U.S. House Committee on Education and Workforce, "The Low-Wage Drag on Our Economy, Wal-Marts low wages and their effect on taxpayers and economic growth," Report by the Democratic members, May 2013. http://democrats.edworkforce.house.gov/sites/democrats. edworkforce.house.gov/files/documents/WalMartReport-May2013.pdf

(Elizabeth) **Warren** for Senate, "The Tax Code Is Rigged," http://elizabethwarren.com/blog/corporateinversions, August 1, 2014.

Scott **Winship**, "Income Inequality is Good For The Poor," *The Federalist,* November 5, 2014.

Christopher **Witko**, "Campaign Contributions, Access and Government Contracting," *Oxford Journals: The Journal of Public Administration Research and Theory 21(4),* 2011.

Tim **Worstall**, "Fantastical Nonsense About WalMart, The Waltons And $7.8 Billion In Tax Breaks," *Forbes*, April 14, 2014.

Katie **Zezima**, "Everything you need to know about the VA — and the scandals engulfing it," *The Washington Post*, May 30, 2014.

Miscellaneous

Ken **Burns**, "Lewis & Clark, The Journey of the Corps of Discovery" (Video documentary), *Public Broadcast Service PBS,* Washington, DC, 1997.

William R. **Cook**, *Tocqueville and the American Experiment* (Video, Chantilly, VA: The Great Courses, The Teaching Company, 2004).

infoplease: Milestone cases in Supreme Court History, consulted February 27, 2016. http://www.infoplease.com/ipa/ A0101289.html

Edwin **Lyngar** on *twitter* @Edwin_Lyngar, published in *SALON*, July 16, 2014.

OpenSecrets.org: "Lobby," consulted October 14th, 2015.
https://www.opensecrets.org/lobby/

The **Rachel Maddow Show,** MSNBC, November 20, 2014.

Stephen **Nass** and C. **Ingraham**, Diagram: *"Gerrymandering explained"*, in *The Washington Post"*, March 1, 2015.

Public Broadcast System, "PBS-Healthcare Crisis, Healthcare Timeline," www.pbs.org/healthcarecrisis/history.htm

Daniel N. **Robinson**, *"American Ideals: Founding a 'Republic of Virtue'"* (Video lectures), The Great Courses, The Teaching Company, Chantilly, VA., 2004.

Walmart Gross Profit, "Walmart Revenue, Profits - WMT Annual Income Statement" (NYSE:WMT),
https://amigobulls.com/stocks/WMT/income-statement/annual

David **Wassermann**, Chart: *"Republicans control these six states, all of which supported President Obama in 2012"*, Cook Political Report.

Wikipedia: "Code of Hammurabi," consulted April 14, 2015.

Wikipedia: "Flat tax", consulted January 18, 2018.

Wikipedia: "Household Income in the United States," consulted May 28, 2015.

Wikipedia: "Objectivism by Ayn Rand" [consulted November 9, 2015].
https://en.wikipedia.org/wiki/Objectivism_(Ayn_Rand).

Wikipedia: "Reagonomics," consulted May 20, 2015.
http://en.wikipedia.org/wiki/Reaganomics

Wikipedia: "Swiftboating".

Wikipedia: "The Great Society," consulted April 23, 2015.

Wikipedia: "The United States presidential election 2000." Consulted June 22, 2015. https://en.wikipedia.org/wiki/ United States presidential election, 2000

Wikipedia: "Welfare, USA," consulted January 24, 2016.
https://en.wikipedia.org/wiki/Welfare#United_States

The three graphs in the book are printed in black and white. The original graphs are in color and will be published in the e-book as well as on the webpage: www.restore-trust.com.

June 2018

Made in the USA
Columbia, SC
20 August 2018